Glorious Covenant

Our Journey Toward
Better Covenant Theology

Stan Newton

Foreword by Dr. Jonathan Welton

Glorious Covenant:
Our Journey Toward Better Covenant Theology

Dr. Stan Newton

Copyright © by Dr. Stan Newton

ISBN: 978-1-61529-159-5

Vision Publishing
1672 Main St. E 109
Ramona, CA 92065
1-800-9-VISION
www.booksbyvision.com

Unless otherwise indicated, all Scripture quotations are from the Holy Bible, English Standard Version, copyright 2001 by Crossway Bibles, a publishing ministry of Good News Publishers. Used by permission.

Thanks

I wish to thank those who helped in bringing <u>Glorious Covenant</u> to print. First, I am grateful for the readers of <u>Glorious Kingdom</u> who sent their encouragement to write on the subject of covenant. Second, thank you to Burton and Patricia Roberts, Randall S. Newton and Virginia Newton who helped with editing and proof reading. Third, thank you Lindsay Stefanov, Stephan Ivov Stepanov and those who assisted from Life in Glory Church, Stara Zagora Bulgaria for designing the cover. Fourth, to Dr. Stan DeKoven for publishing this book and to his staff, especially Kathy Smith. And last, I thank you the reader. You are the final vote if Glorious Covenant strengthens the Church to walk in the realities of the New Covenant.

Stan Newton

Dedication

In honor of my four grandchildren, Caleb, Ava, Joshua, and Amelie. My prayer for you is a life filled with joy, finding purpose in the Kingdom of God, and always experiencing God's love. Walk in grace and freedom!

Endorsements for Glorious Covenant

Dr. Stan Newton is passionate about teaching the word of God with accuracy. Living and serving in Eastern Europe as a missionary teacher, he has seen firsthand the problems endemic in the church caused by wrong-headed theology. This is especially seen in the understanding of most Europeans, and frankly, most Westerners, in regards to the issue of God's covenants, and especially the covenant we now enjoy in Christ.

In his outstanding book, *Glorious Covenant*, Dr. Newton systematically and with sensitivity analyses the four primary views on God's covenant, and presents convincingly the case for a Better Covenant Theology, a theology rooted in the Kingdom of God and in the finished work of Christ. I highly endorse this excellent work, which will undoubtedly become a textbook in the worldwide educational system of Vision International University and in other institutions as well.

Stan E. DeKoven, Ph.D.
President
Vision International University and
The International Training and Education Network

It is my recommendation that Dr. Stan Newton needs to consider including the following disclaimer at the front of his new book, Glorious Covenant:

"Caution: Reading this book could be damaging to your current theology and negative worldview! Readers have been known to experience greatly elevated, and positive levels of vision for Planet Earth and the Kingdom of God's influence upon it. Symptoms include, but are not limited to, a fixation on a more pivotal and magnified Cross, an enlarged Jesus, a shrinking devil, and flashing images of an ever-increasing, Glorious Kingdom of God!".... I'm just saying!

Pastor Ralph Lowe
Senior Pastor of Legacy Church
Meridian, Idaho

One of the most misunderstood concepts in the modern-day church is the concept of Covenant Transition. Jesus and the early disciples lived in a period of time when one covenant (the Old Covenant) was coming to an end, and a transition was taking place into a New and Better Covenant. That's what the book of Hebrews is all about; in fact, that's what much of the New Testament is all about - and it is also what *Glorious Covenant* (Stan Newton's follow-up book to his equally important work, *Glorious Kingdom*) is all about. Stan is able to take complex ideas and share them in easy to follow language. Do yourself a favor and absorb the contents of this book, because once you know that the Old Covenant has fully and finally passed away, and you live only under a New and Better Covenant of Grace, everything will change in the way you see God, yourself, and your world.

Dr. Martin I Trench
Lead Pastor, author, and teacher.
Edmonton, Alberta, Canada

I view *Glorious Covenant* as a wonderful in-depth study, follow up and extension to Dr. Stan Newton's previous work *Glorious Kingdom*. Not only does Dr. Stan challenge the mind-sets and thought processes of believers throughout this writing, he also encourages and inspires with relevant present day truth; written in such a way that allows the reader to easily learn and gain understanding. Dr. Stan does a brilliant job joining Covenant and Eschatology together, laying a firm foundation pertaining to the importance of both being understood by all believers, from the perspective of presently living in a New and Better Covenant with Better Promises.

Dr. Stan Newton has given his life to the teaching and demonstrating of the gospel of the kingdom and holds revelatory truths only received through walking miles down roads very few believers have chosen to travel. It is both an honor and a privilege to endorse the material presented in this book. Not in the sense of simply endorsing another good book full of relevant information but to endorse a biblical New Covenant blueprint necessary for the growth and maturity of the universal church. *Glorious Covenant* is a clarion sound of truth; declaring to all those who read its pages, "This is the way, walk in it." As Dr. Stan Newton continues to progress in the revelation of Christ, His church and His kingdom, I'm delighted to progress forward, learning with him in this never-ending quest for true authentic apostolic understanding for the sole purpose of equipping the saints for effective works of service unto the Lord.

Paul L. Graves
Founder, Bible to Life Ministry
Durban North, South Africa
Author, "Every Believer's Authority"

Stan Newton is one of many voices challenging our traditional understanding of the new covenant. He takes us through the different views in the Protestant Church and shows why they fall short of what the Scriptures teach. Stan advocates for what he calls Better Covenant Theology. He contends for our complete freedom from the Law of Moses and any other man-contrived systems of rules that churches create. Grace is the essence of the Better Covenant and the more the Church embraces this essence the healthier she will be. He implores the Church to not become polarized over doctrinal disagreements, but rather to walk in the Law of Christ, which is Love.

Joe McIntyre
Founder and Senior Minister
Word of His Grace Church
and the Healing Centre www.wordofhisgracechurch.org
Empowering Grace Ministries
President, Kenyon's Gospel Publishing Society www.kenyons.org

Glorious Covenant unlocks the heart of Papa God for His creation. Dr. Stan's 'Glorious Kingdom' and 'Glorious Covenant', are the dynamic duo in understanding how to shift eschatological paradigms in a maze of 'last days' theology. In G.C. Stan unlocks the gifts of Papa God's heart for humanity empowering Believers to thrive in the Father's increasing Kingdom by living in Covenant participation.

There are theologians that write from intellectual Biblical knowledge then there are those like Stan who write from the wisdom of the heart. I have admired and deeply appreciated Stan's pioneering work in building foundations for this paradigm shift. The depth of Dr. Stan's wisdom comes from decades of faithful study and divine revelation that brings scripture to life in the pulpits of domestic and international ministries alike. God's faith in and through Dr. Newton has been a proven instrument of transformation in the community of God's people.

Glorious Covenant PROVIDES the ONE - TWO foundational punch cementing the shift in paradigms as Believers learn to live from this joyful revelation and participate in our Glorious Kingdom Covenant.

Rev. Ron R. Peretti
Hope Center the church Puyallup, Washington

Table of Contents

Foreword

Dr. Jonathan Welton

As I studied the topic of the "end-times" over the years, I became convinced that the main focus of Biblical Eschatology was the shift from the Old Covenant to the New Covenant. It was from this perspective that I wrote the book Raptureless. It was along these same lines that my friend Dr. Newton wrote his work, The Glorious Kingdom.

After delving into the end-times for over a decade, I became obsessed with understanding the biblical covenants. Having read through the major works on the subject, I came to the same conclusion that Dr. Newton puts forth in this book. There are currently three schools of understanding covenants: Covenant Theology, Dispensationalism, and New Covenant Theology. Yet all of these systems of interpretation have serious challenges to account for. As I came to this realization the Holy Spirit began to release a fresh revelation, a fresh understanding of the New Covenant that Jesus created.

This new revelation is in its infancy, yet it has been established as "Better Covenant Theology." BCT as it is also known, was officially introduced to the world on April 9th, 2013 at The Welton Academy in Rochester, New York and has been rapidly increasing in acceptance since.

Of all the authors that could run with BCT, I am honored to have the prestigious Dr. Stan Newton write the second book in existence on the topic of Better Covenant Theology. He brings fresh light and perspective to a fresh move of the Holy Spirit in our day. I cannot recommend this work more highly!

As the Apostle Paul wrote in 2 Corinthians 3, this New Covenant is surpassingly glorious, everlasting, and makes us righteousness! This

New Covenant actually unveils the heart of God the Father and reveals Him from the darkness and confusion of the Old Covenant. As we gaze upon God without the Old Covenant in the way, we are transformed into his image with increasing glory!

Dr. Jonathan Welton

Best-Selling Author of School of the Seers and Raptureless
Founder of The Welton Academy

(August 11, 2015)

Introduction

God's people in ancient times were on a journey. They were heading somewhere. So are we. The church today is on a journey; from bondage to freedom; from law to grace. A few in the Old Testament like Abraham and David knew the final destination while others stumbled along. As we read the story of salvation (God and people coming together in relationship) we notice God works on the level of the people. He meets them in their experience and culture and moves them forward. It is a long journey. From Abraham to Jesus was several thousand years. There are high times and low times. Times of great celebrations and seasons of doubt and exile. Men like David jumped beyond their times and experienced God in extraordinary ways. They used God's Laws not as limitations but as a springboard to the future. Then, there are times when rebellion against the rules becomes so strong God uses severe discipline. The core structure which connects the generations is covenant. God uses covenant to move his people closer to the final goal. God is a God of covenants. Christians have a covenant. This covenant was established over 2,000 years ago by Jesus. Sadly many Christians are only vaguely aware of this glorious covenant and the freedoms it brings. This must change and my hope is these pages will assist many on their personal journey to freedom.

Reading our Bible should teach us one thing; covenant is important to God. The covenants of God are the foundation from which the story unfolds. They are the blueprints of God. Ever since the story began in Genesis we get glimpses of where we are going. We see our destiny in each successive covenant. They reveal the heart of God for relationship with his people; his desire for a family reflecting his glory on the earth.

The problem begins with our basic understanding of the word 'covenant.' When a person buys a home in a gated community or a subdivision there are often 'covenants.' The covenant contains what we CANNOT do! You cannot jack up your car in the front driveway, remove the wheels and leave it sitting all winter. You cannot park your boat in front of your house. So we begin with a negative view of covenants; a list of restrictions. There is nothing in the "covenant document" about having a relationship with the Homeowners Association. Just rules! Pay your dues and obey the rules! Bible covenants are more than God providing a list of rules. It contains rules but its objective is creating a people to walk with God. It creates relationship.

As followers of Jesus it is important we understand covenant. Sadly most are left to piece together any understanding from what they experienced over a life time; resulting in a mixture of ideas, blurring of the biblical covenants and resulting in more bondage than freedom. It is time for God's people to walk in what is ours, a wonderful, new, better and glorious covenant.

God is working in his church to create a people committed to his Son and willing to work to advance his kingdom. Two primary themes in Scripture lead us; covenant and kingdom. We do not choose one or the other. We do not move from kingdom into covenant, or the reverse. The kingdom of God flows through the new covenant.

Confusion reigns in a number of churches. In one place tattoos are condemned as "forbidden by the Bible" while in other places they are almost required. A few Christians still maintain Saturday as the Sabbath, while others treat every day the same. Are certain foods to be avoided by believers? Should we stop serving 'pulled pork' at our church potlucks? Is our Christian faith a matter of following rules? Where do we find these rules? Does the New Testament replace one set of rules for a new set?

How we understand 'covenant' is key for practical everyday living and vital for understanding how we proceed to advance the kingdom of God on earth. Far too many Christians live in confusion which results in bondage. Local churches create additional 'laws' for their members in order to keep separate from the world. Sixty years ago attending a sports event was a sin; in fact almost any activity outside the church was suspect. Forty years ago most Evangelical churches taught attending a theater to see a film was sin, dancing was a sin, women should not cut their hair or wear jewelry; and the list goes on. Over time these same churches have changed their minds about what is sin. We seem to be without guidelines for Christian behavior, our worship, or how to walk in freedom. Glorious Covenant Christians focus their life not on 'overcoming sin' or 'putting the flesh to death' but on walking a Spirit-filled and Spirit-lead life. It is not about rules at all, it is allowing Christ to live through us in the power of the Holy Spirit. How did the church get so far away? We have created a Christian lifestyle based more on old covenant principles than new.

There are a number of paths available in writing a book on covenant. The subject is difficult to cover in a single volume. A study of the biblical covenants is one option, yet these are more universally understood and numerous books available. Another path is to concentrate on the blessings of the covenant and find new ways to make the covenant effective in our lives. This would focus on financial blessings, physical healing and other personal blessings. Again, this road is well traveled, especially in Pentecostal/ Charismatic churches.

The subject of forgiveness of sin through the cross of Jesus is central to any New Testament theology. But since it is well documented and we have literally thousands of books on soteriology, this is not a focus here. The road which is less traveled is contrasting covenants from a redemptive-historical perspective; which points us to theology. How do covenants help in understanding the bigger picture of Scripture? How does covenant affect the daily life of Christians? Having studied the biblical landscape of covenants and their various interpreters, I and others have realized none of the established doctrines fit the revelation we are receiving. We need an alternative. We need a fresh perspective on the larger question of how the old and new covenants relate and how one flows into the other.

I have taken liberty to highlight in bold certain words in Scripture and in quotes. This is my choice to frame points of emphasis.

There are presently three views on covenant. As I have studied each one and compared them with Scripture, all fall short. There are aspects of each which are helpful. Yet, we must strive for greater clarity. We need help and this book is one small candle to lighten the dusk many Christians live in.

[Author's note: As far as I know, the term "Better Covenant Theology" was first used by Dr. Jonathan Welton, author and founder of Welton Academy. His book, <u>Understanding the Whole Bible: The King, The Kingdom, and the New Covenant</u> is a must-read for anyone desiring greater knowledge of Better Covenant Theology. After reading my first draft he gave the go-ahead to use the term, "Better Covenant Theology." Therefore, I use the term knowing building a new system of theology takes time and is normally a collaborative effort. With his blessing, I use the term knowing ours is a journey and this is only an introduction. Corrections and additions are certain to happen as we unveil this great biblical subject of covenant; the better covenant.]

Section One – Our Starting Point

Chapter 1

Our Choices

God's Glorious Kingdom flows through his Glorious Covenant. When kingdom and covenant meet in the New Testament we must refocus to avoid blurred vision. All attempts to bring aspects of the old covenant into the new results in doctrinal weakness and practical craziness. Likewise, our understanding of covenant must match the sweeping changes from the old covenant. The end of an era has come (last days) and the fresh start for God's people is portrayed in such drastic language, the Apostle Paul calls believers a "new creation." This sets us apart from people of the old creation; the old covenant.

Once Christians realize we are establishing a kingdom built by Jesus and not by Moses, our lives, our churches and our nations will be on a healthy path. God wants change on the earth and it begins with the church. Confusion concerning the nature of covenant results in a weak and ineffective church majoring on minor issues. Time has arrived for a fresh look at covenant in Scripture.

Jeremiah prophesied a new covenant. It is not a revision of the old; it is not Moses 2.0. The new covenant is entirely new. The old world is gone and a better covenant has come. When a person comes to Christ in salvation their life enters a new existence; old things have passed away and everything becomes new (II Cor. 5:17). Our struggles come from a lack of knowledge and experiential faith of the covenant we live in. The wind of the Spirit is flowing across the church and bringing fresh awareness of who we are in God. Then, from this new covenant identity will flow God's purpose in his kingdom.

A people of the kingdom is coming forth. The church is witnessing a shift away from sensationalism about the end times to a kingdom understanding. We are seeing God's purpose as renewing and saving nations not their destruction. These kingdom people are empowered by the covenant they walk in; the new covenant established by Jesus. If we are unsure about covenant it will affect the application of our victorious eschatology.

Our covenant through Christ is made effective through the Holy Spirit. The Spirit of God is the missing element in covenant discussions. Without the Spirit we are reduced to Bible thumping, finger pointing, endless conjectures and an ever increasing list of rules. When we think parts of the old covenant remain intact, it holds back the church. The church must embrace the power of the Spirit so we can walk in new covenant life. We must allow the Spirit to show us the greater reality of covenant.

When leaders talk of Covenant we often get theological verbiage which for a majority of Christians is not helpful. Many Evangelicals are exposed to Dispensational Theology but beyond that it gets foggy. The Dispensationalist views of the covenant are totally unacceptable because they teach the new covenant as strictly for Israel and possibly a minor sense for Christians. They see the great covenants of Abraham and David primarily for the future, in a 1,000 year millennial kingdom. The dispensational concept mixes eschatology and covenant to create a system where most biblical promises are postponed for the future. They are correct in seeing unity between eschatology and covenant; their failure is seeing which people receive the new covenant and the timing by which it happens. Dispensational teaching gets the covenants wrong because it wrongly interprets the age of the kingdom. This leaves the church longing for Jesus to come and establish his reign. We sing "The King is Coming" because we do not believe he is King now. Christians are told the commission to disciple the nations will not be accomplished. Only when Jesus is seated on a physical throne in Jerusalem will this occur.

We are called to have lasting influence in our world. Just as many have left a future kingdom mindset we now are departing a failed understanding of dispensational thinking of covenant. The tide has turned against Dispensational Eschatology and its view of covenant. Where should we look to find a biblically based structure of salvation history? Where do we turn to understand the relationship between the Old and New Testament? The other alternative is traditional "Covenant Theology." Yet, as we examine Covenant Theology it also fails to deliver a revelation which fits a Spirit-filled life along with a "Victorious Kingdom" view. It creates a unified covenant of grace beginning in Genesis which removes much of the newness of the new covenant. It mixes Old Testament law with New Testament grace. It brings Mosaic Law and New Testament Grace into the same covenant. Traditional Covenant Theology does not work for many of us. It diminishes the cross—despite their claim it does not—and overly emphasizes Old Testament law. We may like the name "Covenant Theology" but once we open the box we are disappointed. Do we have other choices?

Recently a group of Baptists created a third alternative called New Covenant Theology (NCT). Much of what is being discovered is a breath of fresh Scriptural air (compared to the other two). It stresses the newness of the new covenant. It teaches once the new covenant was established we have a new law; the law of Christ. There is lot to be recommended from New Covenant Theology. Yet I see a major problem which I believe will be their theological Achilles heel; their desire to keep covenant separate from eschatology. When they proclaim even dispensationalists can adopt NCT, it reveals a flaw which is too big to fix.

Covenant and Eschatology belong to each other. The Kingdom of God flows through the new covenant. New Covenant Theology is a good beginning but falls short. When eschatology is divorced from covenant, then, our understanding of both covenant and eschatology is marred.

Major positions on covenant

1. Dispensational Theology

2. Covenant Theology

3. New Covenant Theology

I will not fully examine the first three positions from a historical, theological or exegetical point of view; that would take a book for each position. The chapters on Dispensationalism, Covenant Theology and New Covenant Theology will be brief (in comparison with what should be said). The reason for their inclusion is to understand each one and see where changes must be made. Once we finished reviewing we will begin the journey to locate in Scripture what I believe is the life enhancing, freedom giving, hope filled, love centered, legalistic free, and relationship oriented; Spirit led "Better Covenant Theology."

4. Better Covenant Theology

Chapter 2

The Covenants of Dispensationalism

Christians from Evangelical Churches are aware of dispensationalism because of their eschatology. From this 19th Century scheme we ended up with the rapture, a separate covenant for modern Israel, and the constant reminder we are living in the "last days." It produces an escapist mentality and as a result the church continues to decline in cultural influence. The message has been simple; we (church) are here to save your soul for heaven. "We don't care about the Earth; God wants to destroy it anyway." The message of Dispensationalism places the church within history but it plays no significant role in history.

Dispensational theology rarely speaks of covenants but renames the flow of biblical history into dispensations. It remains a mystery to me how these dispensations are picked and how others are overlooked. Dispensational eschatology is based upon the final two dispensations; Church and Kingdom. The others are less known: the dispensations of Innocence, Conscience, Human Government, Promise, and Law. The entire story of biblical history then fits within the flow of these dispensations. Each one is separate, there is no "progressive revelation" leading us to Jesus and his church. The church is a mystery not known in the Old Testament.

Each dispensation ends with failure and judgment. Therefore, not only will the church fail in its mission but the kingdom will also fail. Dispensationalists provide us with nothing more than a handbook for failure. Only after human history is completed is there any victory. It does not offer any reasonable solution to comprehend a flow of salvation history through the Bible.

Less known is how their dispensational eschatology and their view of covenants have merged, producing a number of wayward theological children. The doctrinal children of dispensationalism have corrupted the church. They made the Holy Apostolic Church of Jesus plan B in God's eternal purposes. The doctrine of dispensationalism is finally losing ground in the church, yet, there are multitudes of sincere believers trapped within its walls. They need a concise, clear and biblical path to escape this theological nightmare.

A starting place to unravel dispensationalism and its view of covenant is found in Jeremiah 31. This famous prophecy reveals the structure of their covenant view and how it affects New Testament interpretation.

Jeremiah 31:31-34

Behold, the days are coming, declares the LORD, when I will make a new covenant with the house of Israel and the house of Judah, ³² not like the covenant that I made with their fathers on the day when I took them by the hand to bring them out of the land of Egypt, my covenant that they broke, though I was their husband, declares the LORD. ³³ For this is the covenant that I will make with the house of Israel after those days, declares the LORD: I will put my law within them, and I will write it on their hearts. And I will be their God, and they shall be my people. ³⁴ And no longer shall each one teach his neighbor and each his brother, saying, 'Know the LORD,' for they shall all know me, from the least of them to the greatest, declares the LORD. For I will forgive their iniquity, and I will remember their sin no more."

Jeremiah uses the words new covenant and it becomes the phrase used most by Jesus and the apostles. Yet, in the Old Testament the exact phrase new covenant is used sparingly; just this single time.

The average Christian recognizes this prophecy refers to what Jesus accomplished on the cross. Jesus said the 'new covenant' is in his blood (Luke 22:20). Israel was under the old covenant and

Christians are under the new covenant. Nevertheless, this common sense approach is not found among dispensational scholars.

Dispensationalists teach that Luke 22:20 and Jeremiah 31:31-34 are different covenants. The reason for this bizarre interpretation is based on their hermeneutic; the prophecy of Jeremiah MUST be taken literally. It is only for the house of Judah and the house of Israel. Therefore, whatever Jesus was talking about, it was NOT a fulfillment of Jeremiah's prophecy. The only option is to say, there are two new covenants. The primary one is for Israel and a second new covenant for the church. An alternative dispensational view is one new covenant but having two administrations. Either way it is forced exegesis.

Charles C. Ryrie is a well-known dispensational scholar. Along with John Darby, C.I Scofield, John Walvoord, and a host of others, Ryrie writes to explain dispensationalism. Concerning the prophecy about a new covenant Ryrie comments.

"The promise of the new covenant "to remove the heart of rebellion" and give us "hearts fully compliant" is not fulfilled today in the experience of believers...Is it true to say that any part of the new covenant as promised in the Old Testament has been inaugurated? Putting all the Old Testament passages together one finds these new covenant promises: (1) putting God's law into Israelites; (2) no necessity to teach His people; (3) forgiveness of Israel; (4) Israel restored to favor and guaranteed everlasting existence; (5) God's Spirit upon the People; (6) material blessing in the land of Israel; (7) peace; (8) God's sanctuary rebuilt. Of course, none of these promises has been inaugurated for the House of Israel and the house of Judah today."[1]

Although Ryrie admits some aspects of the new covenant exists in Christians, they are not fulfillment of the new covenant but merely

---

[1]   Charles C. Ryrie, Dispensationalism, Moody Press, Chicago, Illinois, 1995, p. 171

an early payment of what comes later.[2] The inauguration of the new covenant is future; in the Millennium.

A quick read of Ryrie reveals his approach to Jeremiah. He interprets the prophecy strictly for natural Israel, therefore, Christians are not in view. The consistent literal approach to Scripture which dispensationalists employ is a key reason for such extreme positions of doctrine. Only in rare occasions where the context dictates a symbolic meaning will they alter from a literal approach. Therefore, when Jeremiah says the new covenant is with the house of Judah and the house of Israel, only the bloodline from Abraham is included in the prophecy.

As the story unfolds in the first century a remnant of the house of Israel and the house of Judah embraces Jesus as their Messiah and enters the new covenant. Later gentiles are added and we have the eschatological Israel of God which goes forward. The majority of Jews, following their leaders, rejected Jesus (John 1:11) and therefore, the kingdom was removed from them (Matt. 21:43). This is how the new covenant prophesied by Jeremiah is fulfilled; by the people of the new covenant; the church. We have a new covenant and with it we receive new promises and are the vessels of fulfillment for both the Abrahamic and Davidic covenants. Because of the enthronement of Christ we receive the great promise; all nations will be blessed.

The problem we face with Jeremiah is if we interpret his words literally, then only the bloodline of Jews can receive the new covenant and dispensationalists are right. Yet, if we overly symbolize the prophecy we lose its potency. I see a literal fulfillment taking place here because the church is NOT a symbol of old Israel, the church IS Israel. A better word than literal is biblical. We are not using it as in "our position is biblical and yours is not" but as following the method of interpretation of the early church. We need to learn how the apostolic church of the first century understood this term (new covenant) and other terms. Believing Jews and Gentiles

---

[2]   Ibid.

through the cross and resurrection are made into "one new man (Eph. 2:15)." The new covenant is given to the new eschatological people of God; the glorious church. The reason this newly formed people are eschatological is because they are born in the last days. Once God establishes the new covenant through Jesus he then brings forth a new people which has continuity with the old (first century Jewish remnant) and discontinuity from the old (a new Israel based upon the new covenant).

This eliminates the false accusations of replacement theology because there is continuity from the believing remnant of Jews in the first century with believing Gentiles. Yet, it is proper to say the old covenant is replaced by the new covenant. Jesus was clear in his confrontations with the Jewish leaders; they cannot depend on their bloodline (we are Abraham's children) and remain in covenant with God. Therefore those rejecting their Messiah were removed; alas, replaced. But it is not Gentiles replacing Jews but people "in Christ" (Jews and Gentiles) replacing Moses.

Jeremiah prophesies God will "put my law within them." What law is within us? This is critical and yet I see little discussion about it. For dispensationalists the answer is easy; the Law of Moses. The reason for this is also simple; the law is not for Christians but for natural Israel in the future 1,000-year kingdom. Israel reverts back to the Law of Moses and will have a new temple to worship in. We pick this up in later chapters as the book of Hebrews and Paul in II Corinthians both write about the new covenant and the work of the Spirit.

The author of Hebrews writes to show the supremacy of the new covenant over the old.

Hebrews 8:6-8

But as it is, Christ has obtained a ministry that is as much more excellent than the old as the covenant he mediates is better, since it is enacted on better promises. [7] For if that first covenant had been faultless, there would have been no occasion to look for a second. [8] For he finds fault with them when he says: "Behold, the days are coming, declares the Lord, when I will establish a new covenant with the house of Israel and with the house of Judah.

Here are a few other translations on verse eight:

New Living Translation
> *If the first covenant had been faultless, there would have been no need for a second covenant to replace it.*

International Standard Version
> *If the first covenant had been faultless, there would have been no need to look for a second one.*

Weymouth New Testament
> *For if that first Covenant had been free from imperfection, there would have been no attempt to introduce another.*

The Message

> *But Jesus' priestly work far surpasses what these other priests do, since he's working from a far better plan. If the first plan—the old covenant—had worked out, a second wouldn't have been needed. But we know the first was found wanting, because God said,*

> *Heads up! The days are coming*
> *when I'll set up a new plan*
> *for dealing with Israel and Judah.*
> *I'll throw out the old plan*
> *I set up with their ancestors*
> *when I led them by the hand out of Egypt.*

No matter what translation we use the words of the author are quite clear. The old covenant is gone; it is now replaced by a new covenant. This new covenant is different; it is not like the old. I love the wording of The Message; "I'll throw out the old plan."

The Grace Communion International Commentary explains the need for a new covenant.

"Something was seriously wrong with the Israelite covenant. The people did not have the heart to obey, and God knew it (Deuteronomy 31:16-21, 27-29). Unlike Abraham, they did not believe and were not faithful (Hebrews 3:19). The fault was with the people (Hebrews 8:7-8).

*The Sinaitic covenant had regulations for worship, but it **could not transform the heart or the conscience** (Hebrews 9:9), and yet that is what people really need. The priests had to serve continually, but the high priest could approach God's throne only once a year. This indicated that the sacrificial rituals were not effective (Hebrews 9:7-9; 10:1-3). The people's minds were dull; they could not understand (Matthew 13:14-15; 19:8; 2 Corinthians 4:4), so they remained in the slavery of sin.*

Therefore, God predicted a new covenant. He hinted at it even in the old — he said that, after his people had been sent into captivity because they had broken the covenant, he would gather them again and "circumcise your hearts" (Deuteronomy 4:25-31; 30:4-10).

The prophets predicted a new covenant between God and humans — a new basis of relationship. There would be no need for this new covenant, of course, unless the old were deficient."[3]

The old covenant lacked power to *"transform the heart or the conscience."* The old covenant was not designed as God's final agreement with his people. It was temporary in nature, for a specific people living in a specific time. The old covenant could change behavior but not the heart. There was a few in the Old Testament who possessed a true heart after God, but for the masses, the old covenant did not accomplish a 'circumcision of heart.'

Matthew Henry comments on the grace of the New Covenant:

---

[3]   Grace Communion International, http://www.gci.org

Whereas, by the blood of Christ, a full remission of sins was provided, so that God would remember them no more. God once wrote his laws to his people, now he will write his laws in them; he will give them understanding to know and to believe his laws; he will give them memories to retain them; he will give them hearts to love them, courage to profess them, and power to put them in practice. This is the foundation of the covenant; and when this is laid, duty will be done wisely, sincerely, readily, easily, resolutely, constantly, and with comfort. A plentiful outpouring of the Spirit of God will make the ministration of the gospel so effectual, that there shall be a mighty increase and spreading of Christian knowledge in persons of all sorts. Oh that this promise might be fulfilled in our days. [4]

I appreciate how Henry points to the "outpouring of the Spirit of God' in conjunction how new covenant believers are to walk in God's laws. As we continue to open up this "Better Covenant Theology" the ministry of the Spirit cannot be overlooked or ignored. We do not walk in new covenant truth by old covenant methods. The new covenant is a walk in the Spirit.

A Rebuilt Temple

A key aspect of the dispensationalist covenant view is the rebuilding of the temple for the millennial reign of Jesus. They read Ezekiel's vision of a new temple (ch. 40-48) and envision it being rebuilt so old covenant conditions can again return. Dispensationalism is confusing as its presents the future 1,000-year reign of Christ as being both under old covenant conditions and under the new covenant. When the temple worship resumes they include the Levitical priesthood and restoring animal sacrifices. Alexander Gibb writes:

"During my research, I failed to find any direct quotes from the Book of Ezekiel in the Gospels. Jesus came to the Jews preaching

---

[4]   Concise Commentary on the Whole Bible by Matthew Henry, Thomas Nelson Publishers, Nashville, Tennessee

the Kingdom of God and taught constantly about the many aspects of the Kingdom, often quoting from numerous Old Testament books. If the building of a new temple was a major contributing factor in the overall plan and purpose of God, surely it is reasonable to expect Jesus to have quoted from Ezekiel."[5]

Critics of Gibbs view say an argument from silence is a poor foundation for doctrine. This is true. Nevertheless, Jesus made extensive use of the Old Testament. His many actions and teachings were based upon the Hebrew Scriptures. If the coming of the kingdom includes a rebuilt temple like Ezekiel wrote about, it is difficult to imagine Jesus never mentioning it. I find the argument convincing. Yet, we have more than Jesus' silence. We have passage after passage where Jesus and the apostles spoke about a new temple, one not made with human hands but made from 'living stones' (I Peter 2:5). The times Jesus does speak of the physical temple it is with disparaging words and in the end he proclaims the temple of the Jews will be left *"desolate"* (Matthew 23:38).

To be left desolate can allude to a number of meanings. One is to be left without authority. The physical temple of Israel once stood in the middle of God's people as the center of their faith. It carried the authority of God. Now, with the arrival of the Messiah, a new day has arrived. He will build a new people (a restored eschatological Israel) and the Holy Spirit—the very presence of Yahweh—will be in them. The temple today which carries spiritual authority from God is the church.

The covenant view of dispensationalism steals authority from the church. The church is undermined through faulty exegesis. They remove numerous passages in the New Testament as inapplicable to Christians, because they are not written for Christians but are fulfilled by Israel in the Millennium.

---

[5]   http://searchinsany.hubpages.com

Dispensationalism and the Church

When it comes to the doctrine of the church, dispensationalists stake their claim and get somewhat testy when criticism flies their way. Whereas Covenant Theology unites God's people of all time into one church, dispensationalism in sharp contrast, makes a clear distinction between Israel and the church.

Charles C. Ryrie:

The nature of the church is a crucial point of difference between classic, or normative, dispensationalism and other doctrinal systems. Indeed, ecclesiology, or the doctrine of the church, is the touchstone of dispensationalism.[6]

What separates Covenant Theology from Dispensationalism when it comes to the church is how we understand Israel. Covenant Theology teaches the church fulfills the promises of the Old Testament and becomes New Israel. Whereas, Dispensationalism keeps Israel and the church separate. Ryrie explains:

All non-dispensationalists blur to some extent the distinction between Israel and the church. Such blurring fails to recognize the contrast that is maintained in Scripture between Israel, the Gentiles, and the church. In the New Testament natural Israel and the Gentiles are contrasted. Israel is addressed as a nation in contrast to Gentiles after the church was established at Pentecost (Acts 3:12; 4; 8, 10; 5:21, 31, 35; 21:28). In Paul's prayer for natural Israel (Rom. 10:1) there is a clear reference to Israel as a national people distinct from and outside the church. He also wrote, "Give no offense either to Jews or to Greeks or to the church of God" (I Cor. 10:32). If the Jewish people were the same group as the church or the Gentiles, then certainly there would be no point in the apostle's distinction in this passage... The term Israel continues to be used

---

[6]   Charles C. Ryrie, Dispensationalism, Moody Press, Chicago, Illinois, 1995, p. 123

for the natural (not spiritual) descendants of Abraham after the church was instituted, and it is not equated with the church.[7]

Are you convinced? Or do you find flaws in Ryrie's logic. I do! I say logic and not exegesis because he seems to deduct more from Paul's words than regular exegesis would ever attempt. My reason for providing these quotes is not to build up a straw man in my own words and then tear it down. Too many times we fail to fully understand a theology before dismissing it. It is better for advocates of each system to speak for themselves. We advance truth not by burning down what was never erected. We need honest evaluation of their teaching. And as far as dispensationalism goes, the more they defend their views in writing, the easier it becomes.

Dispensationalists claim "discontinuity" as a foundation for their system of covenant. Simply stated, it means the church is entirely different than the people of God in the Old Testament. Yet, I find their view disingenuous. Why? They correctly point to the church as a "new thing" but within their system much of the old covenant is only postponed and one day comes back into practice. Therefore their approach is more continuous with the old covenant than what they say. When the new covenant is separated from the church and applied to a future time with the nation Israel, it creates huge problems for those wanting a clean break from the old covenant. Dispensationalism and its view of covenants, especially the new covenant, does not work and is difficult to locate in Scripture.

Summary of Covenant from Dispensationalism

- A literal hermeneutic
- Two new covenants
- Israel and the Church always two separate entities
- The kingdom postponed until the Millennium
- The Law of Moses returns in the Millennium.

---

[7]   Ibid. p.127

Chapter 3

Covenant Theology

Defining Covenant Theology is not easy. Baker's Dictionary of Theology gives a simple definition. It says Covenant Theology can be distinguished from other views "By the place it gives to the covenants: (1) the covenant of works, and (2) the covenant of grace." [8]

Although Baker's Dictionary is correct is does not explain the nature of these two covenants. A full definition is provided by a Reformed organization, Christian Publications Resource Foundation:

*Covenant Theology organizes biblical revelation around three unified but distinct covenants: the **Covenant of Redemption**, between the persons of the Trinity in eternity past, in which the Father promises to give a people to the Son as his inheritance, and the Son undertakes to redeem them; the **Covenant of Works**, which God enjoined upon Adam in the Garden, solemnly promising him eternal life if he passed the probationary test in the Garden of Eden (also, many covenant theologians see the covenant given on Mount Sinai as being in some sense a republication of the Covenant of Works); and finally, the **Covenant of Grace**, which God first entered into with Adam immediately after the Fall, when he promised to send a Seed of the woman, who would defeat the tempting serpent (Gen. 3:15). In the Covenant of Grace, God promises a champion to fulfill the broken Covenant of Works as a federal representative of his people, and so to earn its blessings in their behalf. All the later covenants of the bible, such as those which God confirmed to Noah, Abraham, David, and the New Covenant which promises to fulfill these prior covenants in the prophecies of Jeremiah and Ezekiel, are all organically connected, essentially **being different administra-***

---

[8]   Baker's Dictionary of Theology, Grand Rapids, Baker, 1960, p.144

tions of the one eternal Covenant of Grace, which build upon each other and are all brought to completion in the New Covenant which Christ inaugurated with his shed blood.[9]

Our definition of Covenant Theology states there are three covenants; the covenant of Redemption, the covenant of Works and the covenant of Grace. For practical considerations, we will evaluate the final two, since the first is before creation and its existence is not universally supported by covenant theologians.

Simply stated, Covenant Theology has a covenant of works made with Adam in the garden and a covenant of grace which is established after the fall; from Genesis 3:15. Therefore, all covenants following the covenant of grace are not independent covenants but different administrations of the single covenant. Even the new covenant established by Christ is not really new but an administration of the former covenant of grace. The Mosaic Covenant and the New Covenant are not given the status of true covenants but are again covered under the umbrella of the covenant of grace.

New Covenant Theology author Fred G. Zaspel reveals a key fault in this view.

Covenant Theology is designed to show the unity *in God's purpose in human redemption. It is called "covenant" theology not because of an emphasis on the Biblical/historical covenants as such but on* **certain** **theological** **covenants**— *the covenant of redemption, the covenant of works, and the covenant of grace. The covenant of grace is essentially the promise made in Gen.3:15 of the coming deliverer, and all of history is viewed as a progressive unfolding of this covenant. Thus, the New Covenant, in Covenant Theology, is not understood as a* new *covenant actually; it is rather a new "administration" of the covenant of grace, as was the Mosaic*

---

9   What is Covenant Theology, Monergism, Christian Publication Resource Foundation, http://www.monergism.com

Covenant before it. One covenant with various administrations is the essence of Covenant Theology on this point.[10]

Zaspel makes an excellent comment. Covenant Theology does not use the term 'covenant' as referring to the biblical covenants, but to their concepts of a 'theological covenant.' It ignores much of the named covenants in Scripture and creates an entire system around covenants never mentioned. One cannot find the name 'covenant of works' or the 'covenant of grace' in the Bible. This does not make it wrong, but shows a 'forced' understanding of biblical history instead of explaining the actual covenants spoken of in Scripture.

Covenant Theology is more than a set of doctrines; it is a hermeneutic for understanding the Bible. This is the goal of each covenantal position. How do we understand the differences between the Old Testament and the New Testament? How does it all fit together? Why under the Law of Moses were animals sacrificed and under the New Covenant all such sacrifices are eliminated? Understanding the covenant structure of the Bible assists in these types of questions. It simply strives to explain how various parts of the Bible flow together.

History of Covenant Theology

It is common to think John Calvin and his contemporaries created Covenant Theology since it is found mainly in Reformed Churches. But its history is later than the early Reformers. Dispensational author Charles C. Ryrie—no friend of Covenant Theology—agrees that Calvin is not the source of today's Covenant Theology.

Covenant theology does not appear in the writings of Luther, Zwingli, Calvin, or Melanchthon, even though they discussed at length the related doctrines of sin, depravity, redemption, and so on. They had every opportunity to incorporate the covenant idea, but they did not. There were no references to covenant theology in any of the great confessions of faith until the Westminster Confession in

---

[10]   Fred G. Zaspel, A Brief Explanation of "New Covenant Theology," www.biblicalstudie

1647... It is true that Calvin, for instance, spoke of the continuity of redemptive revelation and of the idea of covenant between God and His people, but that was not covenant theology.[11]

According to Ryrie, the early founders of Covenant Theology are Andrew Hyperius (1511-1564), Kaspar Olevianus (1576-1633), and Rafael Eglinus (1559-1622). It was Johannes Cocceius (1603-1669) who in 1648 wrote of two covenants; the covenants of works and grace.[12] So it was over one hundred years after the Reformation when we first hear of the "covenant of works" and the "covenant of grace."

The Covenant of Works

In traditional Covenant Theology, the whole history of the Bible was divided into two major covenant relationships: the covenant of works and the covenant of grace. Neither of these expressions appears in the Bible, but the distinctions form helpful theological categories that reflect the underlying unity of Scripture, much as the term "Trinity" summarizes one essential aspect of the truth of Scripture about God. This dual covenant approach to Scripture finds a clear expression in the Westminster Confession and Catechisms (WCF 7.1-5; 19.1, 6; WLC 31-36, 7).[13]

As we attempt to unravel the covenant of works I find it interesting this particular article admits neither the expressions "covenant of works" nor "covenant of grace" are found in Scripture; but they do find a "clear expression" in the Westminster Confession. It seems our first argument would arrive from Scripture and then second, from historical documents.

The covenant of works came before the covenant of grace. It is the agreement between Adam and God. If Adam by his works

---

[11]   Charles C. Ryrie, Dispensationalism, Moody Press, Chicago, Illinois, 1995, p.186. (The 1995 edition is an revised and expanded version of the original book, Dispensationalism Today written in 1966)

[12]   Ibid.

[13]   Third Millennium Study Bible, http://thirdmill.org

(obedience) kept the commands of God, then, he and all humanity to follow would enjoy life eternal.

Pastor Tom Hicks:

The whole system of Christian doctrine hangs on the two federal (representative) heads of Adam and Christ. Biblical history is structured around the covenant with Adam, or the covenant of works, and the covenant with Christ, or the covenant of grace. Each individual's experience is only properly understood with reference to whether he is "in Adam" or "in Christ." So, I want to begin laying out this "federal scheme" by describing what is meant by the "covenant of works."[14]

According to Covenant Theology the "whole system of Christian doctrine hangs" on structuring the Bible around these two covenants; the first being the covenant of works.

Hicks continues:

God made a covenant with Adam in which He promised Adam justification and eternal life for perfectly fulfilling the law. Had Adam kept the law perfectly, as a federal head, He would have merited justification and eternal life for all of his posterity because they were federally united to him. I don't say that Adam was created in a state of justification and adoption, since God the judge never revokes the life-blessing of justification and because God the Father always preserves His sons and never casts them off, but Adam fell; so, he couldn't have been in a state of justification from the beginning.[15]

As I understand it, if Adam had not disobeyed God, he would then merit justification. Not only Adam but in Adam all of us would be justified, because he is our federal head. Hicks loses me when he

---

[14]   Tom Hicks, Federal Theology the Covenant of Works, 2008, http://lifeinchrist-tom-blogspot.com

[15]   Ibid.

states Adam was not created in a "state of justification" because he did fall, proving he was not previously justified.

What then was Adam's relationship with God before the fall? Is he without sin or not? We see no evidence in Scripture where Adam and Eve were separated from God in the Garden. The covenant—if one chooses to use the term in this occasion (I do not) —seems to be working. Adam and Eve work in beautifying the garden during the day and enjoy fellowship with God in the evening. Covenant Theology in my view goes to an extreme in creating a covenant where none is mentioned and then speculates where and if Adam was justified or not.

If Adam is our federal head and our justification depended on his obedience, how long must Adam continue without committing sin?

Hicks explains:

We're not told explicitly, but it makes sense to say that there was some period of trial or probation through which Adam had to pass in order to merit justification and eternal life. If there were no trial period, after which he would be rewarded with justification and eternal life, then he could never have functioned as "federal" or "representative" head for those who were "in him." [16]

We can only speculate. Maybe if Adam and Eve made it one more day, we all would be living in paradise.

Covenant Theology teaches we are saved by both the covenant of works and the covenant of grace.

Author and theologian R.C. Sproul:

Without Christ's active obedience to the covenant of works, there is no reason for imputation, there is no ground for justification. If we take away the covenant of works, we take away the active obedience of Jesus. If we take away the active obedience of Jesus, we take away the imputation of His righteousness to us. If we take away the

---

[16]   Ibid.

imputation of Christ's righteousness to us, we take away justification by faith alone.[17]

If the covenant of works is essential to our salvation why is it most Christians have never heard of it? This demonstrates layers of complexity within Covenant Theology which I and others cannot unravel. I will not even attempt so. The reason for including these quotes from Covenant Theology advocates is to show it offers little to those experiencing the joy and freedom of living in the new covenant. The new covenant in Christ is our governing relationship about how we relate to God, each other, the church, and how the kingdom functions on earth.

From the covenant of works we now move to Covenant Theology's view of the covenant of grace.

The Covenant of Grace

Theologian and author J. I. Packer write concerning the foundation of Covenant Theology:

First, the gospel of God is not properly understood till it is viewed within a covenantal frame... Second, the word of God is not properly understood till it is viewed within a covenantal frame.[18]

With these two statements I agree. To understand how covenant flows in God's grand story of redemption we need to see the covenant structure from which salvation flows. This should be simple, but Bible teachers over the centuries have created complexity where it is not needed. Even a novice reader of Scripture should be able to see there are two parts to God's story; the Old Testament and the New Testament. Within these testaments are two covenants; the old and the new. With the coming of Jesus the new arrives and the old is no longer needed. Yet both Dispensationalism

---

[17] R. C. Sproul, The Covenant of Works, www.ligonier.org
[18] J. I. Packer, An Introduction to Covenant Theology, The Fig Classic Series, 2012, Electronic Edition

and Covenant Theology places layers of complex logic over what should be clear. The next statement from Packer is an example:

The transition in Eden from the covenant of works to the covenant of grace, and the further transition from all that was involved in the preliminary (old) form of that covenant to its final (new) form brought through the death of Jesus Christ and now administered by him from the throne, are key events in the covenant story.[19]

Please allow me to explain what I believe Packer is saying. I do not desire to insult your intelligence; I explain it because it is key to what I see as a faulty construct of Covenant Theology.

Packer is talking about a "transition in Eden." The covenant of works was God's original agreement with Adam; which was broken. Once the covenant of works came to an end because of Adam and Eve's disobedience, another covenant was instituted; the covenant of grace. So both of Covenant Theology's primary covenants take place in Genesis. Packer continues and explains more about the covenant of grace. He writes about another transition taking place within a single covenant; the covenant of grace. There is a "preliminary" form of the covenant of grace. Although Packer does not state what exactly this "old" form is, by context we can surmise he means the Mosaic covenant or the old covenant. He is not referring back to the covenant of works but to the covenant of grace when he says "that covenant." The "new form" of the covenant of grace is what we have in the work of Christ. The "preliminary" form was the old covenant or the Mosaic covenant.

My main objection to Covenant Theology is how they view the work of Christ and the Mosaic Law under a single covenant. They create an old form and a new form under the covenant of grace in order to somehow distinguish Jesus from Moses. At this junction, in my opinion, Covenant Theology can no longer be the guide to understanding how the Bible flows in its salvation history. The New Testament is clear; the work of Jesus is more than a "new form" of

---

[19]   Ibid.

Moses; it is superior in every way. It is a **New** Covenant, not an extension of a covenant from Genesis.

The Three Divisions of the Mosaic Covenant

What does it mean to be "under the law?" Covenant Theology divides the Law of Moses into three parts; the moral law, the civil law and the ceremonial law. The latter is also called 'religious law.' These three divisions of the law are helpful for their theology as they extend the covenant of grace into the New Testament.

I find no evidence Scripture separates the law into three divisions. No one denies that the Ten Commandments are part of the Mosaic Law. Ask a majority of Christians if these commandments of God are to be obeyed and a majority would agree. Why? Because they are the moral law of God. The moral laws of God are eternal; they are not limited to a single people at a specific time but for all people for all times. Covenant Theology has won over even many dispensationalists on this issue. If a pastor or leader would say the Ten Commandments are not for Christians, the kickback would be tremendous.

Keith Mathison: *The ceremonial laws are now defined in terms of the atoning death of Christ (cf. Heb. 9:11–10:11) rather than the blood of bulls and goats. The moral law, however, — that which sets forth the universal and eternal standards of righteousness — is unchanged. Although it is now written on the hearts of God's people rather than on tablets of stone, this law remains the same.*[20]

Keith Mathison agrees with most Christians the ceremonial laws are fulfilled in the death of Jesus. He says, however, the moral law remains. What about the civil law? A small but vocal group within Covenant Theology accepts a position called Theonomy. This position teaches ALL the Mosaic Law is binding upon Christians, except when it is implicitly stated to be fulfilled in the New

---

[20]   Keith Mathison, The New Covenant, Ligonier Ministries, www.ligonier.org

Testament. Therefore not only the moral law is to be enforced but also the civil law.

If Theonomy was the law of the land today, how much of the Mosaic Law would be enforced? Like any theological system there are various views. I find this quote by theonomist John M. Frame amazing and also disturbing:

There is some confusion in theonomy between present and future application of the law. Often when Bahnsen is pressed as to the difficulty of enforcing theonomy in today's world, he argues that the Mosaic laws should not *be enforced today. They presuppose, he argues, a people who understand and believe the law and who are committed to be God's people. But this idea turns theonomy from a practical present program to a future ideal. Yet the rhetoric of theonomists is often calculated to arouse immediate action. I suspect that few of us would disagree with theonomy if it were simply presented as a future ideal. Sure: if the postmillennial hope is realized and the world-society with its institutions becomes largely Christian, then **most of us would find very attractive the prospect of living under something like the Mosaic civil law.**[21]*

Even if the majority of Mosaic Laws are for the future, when a majority of people are Christian and we have true Christian civilizations, will "*most of us would find very attractive the prospect of living under something like the Mosaic civil law?*" I have serious doubts Christians would find even the civil laws of Moses attractive, let alone the complete corpus of the Mosaic code. Does the prospect of living under the civil laws of Moses excite you? Judge for yourself; here is an example the Mosaic Civil Laws.

190. Not to compel the Hebrew servant to do the work of a slave (Lev. 25:39)
191. Not to sell a Hebrew servant as a slave (Lev. 25:42)
197. Not to sell a Hebrew maid-servant to another person (Ex.

---

[21]   John M. Frame, Frame and Poythress, Penultimate Thoughts on Theonomy, http://www.frame-poythress.org

21:8)
199. To keep the Canaanite slave forever (Lev. 25:46)
205. Not to violate an oath or swear falsely (Lev. 19:12)

212. Not to till the ground in the Sabbatical year (Lev. 25:4)
213. Not to do any work on the trees in the Sabbatical year (Lev.25:4)
220. To assemble the people to hear the Torah at the close of the seventh year (Deut. 31:12)

254. Not to take a bribe (Ex. 23:8)
256. Not to be moved in trying a case, by the poverty of one of the parties (Ex. 23:3; Lev. 19:15)
263. To make a parapet for your roof (Deut. 22:8)
273. Never to settle in the land of Egypt (Deut. 17:16)
279. Not to kidnap any person of Israel (Ex. 20:13)
285. That the Court shall pass sentence of death by decapitation with the sword (Ex. 21:20; Lev. 26:25)
286. That the Court shall pass sentence of death by strangulation (Lev. 20:10)
287. That the Court shall pass sentence of death by burning with fire (Lev. 20:14)
288. That the Court shall pass sentence of death by stoning (Deut.22:24)
289. To hang the dead body of one who has incurred that penalty (Deut. 21:22)
293. To exile one who committed accidental homicide (Num. 35:25)
302. That one who has raped a damsel and has then (in accordance with the law) married her, may not divorce her (Deut. 22:29)
304. To punish the wicked by the infliction of stripes (Deut. 25:2)
305. Not to exceed the statutory number of stripes laid on one who has incurred that punishment (Deut. 25:3)
311. Not to refrain from putting a false prophet to death nor to be in fear of him (Deut. 18:22)

Many of these civil laws can easily be adapted to our times. They deal with basic morality; don't steal, don't cheat people in business, don't lie, etc. The problem is applying all the laws about civil life and government. We can have slaves as long as they are not Hebrews. Canaanite slaves are OK. Are we ready to pass a death sentence by *decapitation*? Then what about *strangulation*, or *burning with fire*? If those are too brutal then we can just crush people's skulls by *stoning*. If a person is guilty of rape, what is the punishment? He is to marry her without any possibility of divorce!

How can we apply *"never settle in the land of Egypt?"* Should all Christians move out of Egypt? And then what about prophecies concerning God's blessings upon Egypt? Also, we are commanded to put false prophets to death. Now, there are many in non-charismatic churches who may not be opposed to this, but again, who is the final authority on who is put to death? As we can see, this type of laws make actual enforcement very problematic in modern society.

Allow me to ask a difficult question: Are all these Laws of Moses really from the heart of God? Are any in conflict with our understanding of the character of God, his very nature? Without questioning the inspiration of Scripture, could it be these Laws for the ancient Hebrews came because of necessity? They were to be a separate nation and therefore needed special protection. It was never God's plan for his people to live for all time under such restrictions. There is a need for biblical scholars to address difficult questions most are afraid to ask. At this stage all I can say is, thank God for the new covenant!

Should Christians keep the Law of Moses? Should we be worshiping on Saturday, refrain from pork ribs and keep a long list of the 613 laws on our refrigerator in case we forget one? No position which claims to be Christian advocates keeping all the Law of Moses (at least that I know).

In a paper by J. Ligon Duncan, III now Chancellor/CEO of Reformed Theological Seminary, Dr. Duncan is critical of Greg

Bahnsen and his position on Theonomy. The paper was given to The Social Science History Association in Atlanta, Georgia. The paper was entitled Moses' Law for Modern Government—The Intellectual and Social Origins of the Christian Reconstructionist Movement. For those desiring an in-depth and academic treatment of Reconstructionism, this is an excellent resource. In this paper Duncan states:

Second, it should be noted that the designation "ceremonial law" is not employed in the Bible, nor is there anything like a comprehensive list of what might fall into such a category of laws. Is it as easy to distinguish civil and ceremonial law in the Torah as Bahnsen seems to suggest? Yet, Bahnsen's argument assumes and proceeds on a readily identifiable set of "ceremonial laws." How does he recognize these? — by his assessment of their character, not by exegetical directive. What is the basis of the category "ceremonial law" then? It is determined descriptively? Third, though he insists that the New Testament allows for no distinction between moral and civil laws, the fact is that the New Testament does indeed make much of the distinction between the Old and New Covenant structure of the kingdom of God. Under the Old Covenant the institutional form of the kingdom of God was the nation-state of Israel. The New Covenant institutional form of the kingdom of God is the church (which is non-national and transnational in its embodiment). This shift provides an important, simple and obvious rationale for the expiration of the judicial law. The civil law of Israel (as the application of God's eternal standards to a particular situation in the history of his kingdom) has now (in the progress of his redemptive economy) passed away with the demise of that state (in its unique role as earthly representative of the rule of God) and the advent of a superior institutional expression of God's rule.

The argument centers on whether the Mosaic Law is one unified set of laws or if there are three aspects of it, namely the ceremonial, civil, and moral laws. If we need to separate the Law of Moses where in the New Testament can we find guidelines for such divisions? For me, when Paul or the other writers speak about not being under the law, it means ALL the Law not just parts of it.

Dr. Duncan makes a good point concerning the kingdom of God and the institutional form it takes under the new covenant. We are not building a society or culture on Old Testament Law. The church now possesses the kingdom and we function and expand the reign of King Jesus by new covenant principles. In case anyone is drawn to Reconstructionism, allow me one more quote. This is a list of laws to which modern nations should apply the death penalty:

One of the primary founders of Christian Reconstructionism is Rousas John Rushdoony. He wrote in The Institutes of Biblical Law that Old Testament law should be applied to modern society and advocates the reinstatement of the Mosaic Law's penal sanctions. Under such a system, the list of civil crimes which carried a death sentence would include homosexuality, adultery, incest, lying about one's virginity, bestiality, witchcraft, idolatry or apostasy, public blasphemy, false prophesying, kidnapping, rape, and bearing false witness in a capital case.[22]

Who would decide on matters of apostasy or false prophesying? Will society turn into a fear based community where we are afraid our neighbors will turn us in for some minor infraction? This is not the glory of God covering the earth. This is not the increase of God's peace in the earth. This is not the kingdom Jesus established.

I imagine most reading this are not interested in Theonomy. Yet, I bring it up because there are a few in the Pentecostal/Charismatic camp which are drawn to it. Theonomy offers an objective standard for measuring the advance of the kingdom and can be a draw for those leery of constant subjectivism. With a normal overdose of subjective worship in P/C camps a dose of objectivity is refreshing. Nevertheless, I would ask at what cost? What theonomy offers in objectivity it takes away with its almost brutal enforcement for those

---

[22]   Durand, Greg Loren, *Reconstructionism's Commitment to Mosaic Penology: Christian Reconstruction and Its Blueprints for Dominion*, Crown rights, retrieved June 10, 2008.

not in compliance with the Law of Moses. Christianity offers transformation from the inside out. We should not be forcing unsaved people lacking personal transformation to behave like mature Christians. Neither should we say the mark of a mature believer is keeping the Mosaic Law because this is not taught in the New Testament. John G. Reisinger, an advocate of New Covenant Theology, makes an intriguing statement:

The only way Covenant Theology can continue "as is" is if Theonomy takes over in Covenant Theology circles, but this seems most unlikely, simply because they cannot secure the use and authority of the sword to enforce their theology in the same manner as did the Puritans. The sword, not open debate, is what kept Covenant Theology in force under the Puritans. The basic presuppositions of Covenant Theology are just assumed to be true; they cannot be established with texts of Scripture. Covenant Theology will only discuss issues in the light of the WCF.[23] This attitude cannot be acceptable to anyone who really takes Sola Scriptura *seriously.[24]*

I highly doubt if Theonomists will become the primary voice for Covenant Theology. Neither Covenant Theology nor its hybrid version of Theonomy works. It forces Old Testament laws on Christians who have been freed from the law. It creates an overreaching covenant of grace where the Laws of Moses and the Laws of Christ are under the same covenant and makes it difficult to know which laws ought to be obeyed. It creates a system and then attempts to force everything to form around it.

Covenant Theology and Salvation

Since Covenant Theology is committed to one comprehensive covenant it seems logical that the way of salvation is the same. Abraham, Moses, David, Jeremiah and all of Israel are saved in exactly the same manner as those living since the day of Pentecost.

---

[23]   Westminster Confession of Faith
[24]   John G. Reisinger, What is New Covenant Theology, http://gospelpedlar.com/articles/bi

The people in the Old Testament were saved through faith by looking forward to the Messiah whereas for two thousand years people have been saved through faith by looking back to the Messiah.

Charles Hodge explains:

From the Scriptures, therefore, as a whole, from the New Testament, and from the Old as interpreted by infallible authority in the New, we learn that the plan of salvation has always been one and the same; having the same promises, the same Savior, the same conditions, and the same salvation.[25]

Dispensationalists are often cited as teaching two ways of salvation; they deny this is part of dispensationalism. L. S. Chafer refutes this charge from covenant theologians when he wrote an article called Inventing Heretics through Misunderstanding:

Are there two ways by which one may be saved? In reply to this question it may be stated that salvation of whatever specific character is always the work of God in behalf of man and never a work of man in behalf of God. This is to assert that God never saved any person or group of persons on any ground than that righteous freedom to do so which the Cross of Christ secured. There is, therefore, but one way to be saved and that is by the power of God made possible through the sacrifice of Christ.[26]

Each side claims the other is wrong about salvation yet both agree salvation is the same throughout Scripture, both in the Old Testament and in the New Testament. When we review New Covenant Theology a different scenario will emerge.

We see that advocates of Covenant Theology are not comfortable in calling the new covenant new. They always attempt to reduce the

---

[25]   Charles Hodge, Systematic Theology, Nelson, 1872, London, p.368
[26]   L. S. Chafer, "Inventing Heretics Through Misunderstanding, Bibliotheca Sacra, 101, July 1944

newness by substituting alternative words. From Third Day Millennium we see this clearly:

Hebrews 8:8 begins an extended quote from Jeremiah 31:31-34. In its original context, Jeremiah's prophecy spoke of a time when the exiled people of Israel and Judah would be restored to the Promised Land and would receive the blessings of God's covenant in all their fullness. Jeremiah's offer of a "new covenant" was an offer of forgiveness for transgressions committed under the covenant as it was administered under Moses (cf. Heb. 9:15) and of restoration to God's favor under that same covenant (Heb. 8:12; Jer. 31:34). **Through Jeremiah, God offered to renew and restore - not replace - his covenant with his people.** *Although traditional translations have favored the term "new," both the Hebrew (Jer. 31:31) and the Greek (Heb. 8:8) words for "new" may be translated "renewed." Owen says, "This covenant was a collection and confirmation of all the promises of grace that had been given to the church since the world began." See WLC 35; BC 7.*[27]

When advocates of Covenant Theology say God offered "To renew and restore—not replace" the old covenant, I wonder what version of Hebrews 8:7 they are reading. The intent of Hebrews is to show the superiority of the new and better covenant to the old. It never says the old needed to be fixed—or renewed—**or anything but replaced.**

Those desiring some type of continuation of old covenant law point to how the law itself is written. The first is written in stone and given to Moses. The second is written in the heart. Yet it is the same law. If this is correct then why do we accept the death of Jesus as the final sacrifice needed for sin? If it is the same law we would be still be under the whole of the Mosaic Law.

Certainly, parts of the old law have passed away, so therefore we need to see how all this works in the new covenant age. We cannot pick and choose which parts of the old we want written in our heart.

---

[27]   Third Millennium Study Bible, Notes on Hebrews 8:8-12, http://thirdmill.org/begin.asp

One hint in the direction we are headed: when there is a change in covenants there is also a change in laws (Heb. 7:12).

Before moving on to the third alternative, I found an extensive side-by-side comparison of Dispensational and Covenant Theology. The author is unknown. For the record, if you provide valuable information; put your name on it. If you advocate one of these positions and find some points are not representative of your view, you may be right; yet, because of its exhaustive nature it provides a grand view of the differences and based on my study over the years, I find it largely accurate.

DISPENSATIONAL THEOLOGY (Lewis S. Chafer, John Walvoord, Tim LaHaye, John Nelson Darby, C.I. Scofield)	COVENANT THEOLOGY (Charles Hodge, Loraine Boettner, Louis Berkhof, John Murray, B.B. Warfield)
1. May be Arminian or modified Calvinist. Almost never 5-point Calvinist.	1. Always Calvinist. Usually 5-point.
2. Stresses *rigidly* 'literal' interpretation of the Bible.	2. Accepts 'normal' interpretation of the Bible text (allows both literal and figurative)
3. Usually does not accept the idea of the 'Analogy of Faith.'	3. Almost always accepts the idea of The "Analogy of Faith."
4. 'Israel' always means only the literal, physical descendants of Jacob.	4. "Israel" may mean either literal, physical descendants of Jacob or the figurative, spiritual Israel, depending on context.
5. 'Israel of God' in Gal. 6:16 means physical Israel alone.	5. "Israel of God" in Gal. 6:16 means spiritual Israel, parallel to Gal. 3:29; Rom. 2:28-29; Phil. 3:3.
6. God has two peoples with two separate destinies: Israel (earthly) and the Church (heavenly).	6. God has always had only one people; the Church gradually developed.
7. The Church was born at Pentecost.	7. The Church began in O.T. Acts 7:38 and reached fulfillment in the N.T.
8. The Church was not prophesied as such in the O.T. but was a hidden mystery until the N.T.	8. There are many O.T. prophecies of the N.T. Church.

9. All O.T. prophecies for "Israel" are for literal Israel, not the Church.	9. Some O.T. prophecies are for the literal nation of Israel, others are for spiritual Israel.
10. God's main purpose in history is literal Israel.	10. God's main purpose in history is Christ and secondarily the Church.
11. The Church is a parenthesis in God's program for the ages.	11. The Church is the culmination of God's saving purpose for the ages.
12. The main heir to Abraham's covenant was Isaac and literal Israel.	12. The main heir to Abraham's covenant was Christ and spiritual Israel.
13. There was no eternal Covenant of Redemption within the Trinity.	13. The eternal Covenant of Redemption was within the Trinity to effect election.
14. There was no Covenant of Works with Adam in the Garden of Eden.	14. God made a conditional Covenant of Works* with Adam as representative for all his posterity.
15. There was no Covenant of Grace concerning Adam.	15. God made a Covenant of Grace with Christ and His people, including Adam.
16. Israel was rash to accept the Covenant at Mt. Sinai.	16. Israel was right to accept the Covenant Mt. Sinai.
17. The 'New Covenant' of Jer. 31:31- 34 is only for literal Israel and is not the New Covenant of Lk. 22:20.	17. The "New Covenant" of Jer. 31 is the same as in Lk. 22; both are for spiritual Israel according to Heb. 8.
18. God's program in history is mainly through separate dispensations.	18. God's program in history is mainly through related covenants.
19. Some Dispensationalists have said that O.T. sinners were saved by works.	19. No man has ever been saved by works, but only by grace.
20. Most Dispensationalists teach that men in the O.T. were saved by faith in a revelation peculiar to their dispensation, but this did not	20. All men who have ever been saved have been saved by faith in Christ as their sin-bearer, which has been

include faith in the Messiah as their sin-bearer.	progressively revealed in every age.
21. The O.T. sacrifices were not recognized as the Gospel or types of the Messiah as sin-bearer, but only seen as such in retrospect.	21. O.T. believers believed in the Gospel of Messiah as sin-bearer mainly by the sacrifices as types and prophecies.
22. The Holy Spirit indwells only believers in the dispensation of Grace, not O.T. and not after the Rapture.	22. The Holy Spirit has indwelt believers in all ages, especially in the present N.T. era, and will not be withdrawn.
23. Jesus made an offer of the literal Kingdom to Israel; since Israel rejected it, it is postponed.	23. Jesus made only an offer of the spiritual Kingdom, which was rejected by literal Israel but has gradually been accepted by spiritual Israel.
24. O.T. believers were not in Christ, not part of the Body or Bride of Christ.	24. Believers in all ages are all "in Christ" and part of the Body and Bride of Christ.
25. The Law has been abolished.	25. The Law has 3 uses: to restrain sin in society, to lead to Christ, and to instruct Christians in godliness. The ceremonial Laws have been abolished; the civil laws have been abolished except for their general equity; the moral laws continue.
26. O.T. laws are no longer in effect unless repeated in the N.T.	26. O.T. laws are still in effect unless abrogated in the N.T.
27. The Millennium is the Kingdom of God. Dispensationalists are always Pre-Millennial and usually Pre-Tribulational.	27. The Church is the Kingdom of God. Covenanters are usually Amillennial, sometimes Pre-Millennial or Post-Millennial, rarely Pre-Tribulational.

28. The O.T. animal sacrifices will be restored in the Millennium.	28. The O.T. sacrifices were fulfilled and forever abolished in Christ.
29. The Millennium will fulfill the Covenant to Abraham. Israel has a future.	29. Christ fulfilled the Covenant to Abraham. Some Covenanters believe in a future for literal Israel, most don't.
30. David will sit on the Millennial throne in Jerusalem.	30. Christ alone sits on the throne. Saints rule under Him.

Which position reflects better your position? On the dispensational side I found only a few points I agree with. On the other side, Covenant Theology, I agreed with many points. Yet for the reason provided, I find Covenant Theology not in agreement with the teaching in the New Testament and certainly for anyone in Pentecostal or Charismatic churches.

At this stage if there are only two choices; Covenant Theology wins. So Dispensationalism loses round one and is dropped. Covenant Theology moves to the next round, to take on New Covenant Theology.

Chapter 4

New Covenant Theology

The new kid on the theological block is New Covenant Theology (NCT). Since this third alternative is fairly new and has yet to produce neither a systematic theology nor a final statement of beliefs, we can only trace the points as they are developing.

Theopedia provides a place to begin understanding New Covenant Theology:

New Covenant Theology is a technical term referring to a theological view of redemptive history primarily found in Baptist circles and contrasted with Covenant theology and Dispensationalism. It has been assumed that one has only two primary options in understanding the structure of the Bible in evangelical Christianity — Covenant Theology (coming out of the Reformation) or Dispensationalism. However, proponents see what has come to be called New Covenant Theology as middle ground with a biblical basis of understanding.

Proponents maintain that the primary thrust of New Covenant Theology is the recognition of a promise-fulfillment understanding of Scripture. They suggest that whereas "Dispensationalism cannot get Israel and the church together in any sense whatsoever, and Covenant Theology cannot get them apart" (Reisinger, 19), New Covenant Theology finds the realization of all that the Old Covenant typified in the New Testament church (Covenant Theology, in contrast, merely levels the playing field and identifies them for all intents and purposes). The Mosaic economy is viewed as a temporal, conditional covenant that has been forever replaced by the glory of the New Covenant (2 Corinthians 3).[28]

---

[28]   Theopedia is a growing online evangelical encyclopedia of biblical Christianity

From this beginning we can glean several stating points. First, New Covenant Theology is a theological term carving out a third alternative for the understanding of redemptive history and how covenant functions in Scripture. It should not to be confused with studies in New Testament theology, which is a broad review of basic doctrines found in the New Testament.

Second, New Covenant Theology is a movement primarily in Baptist circles. This centers their studies within Evangelicalism and needs to be taken serious as a biblical option by conservation scholarship.

Third, New Covenant Theology sees Scripture in a promise-fulfillment model, with the old covenant promises being fulfilled by Jesus in the new covenant. As we will see, this is slightly tricky as to how it is fleshed out.

New Covenant Theology author Fred Zaspel:

New Covenant Theology (NCT) is but one recent attempt to move forward in this quest. As yet it is less a settled theology than a movement still in the shaping by men who agree that the question has not yet been finally answered by either of the major competing schools of interpretation—Dispensational Theology and Covenant Theology. There are still disagreements among us on several details, such as the questions of the future of ethnic/national Israel and the Millennium. "[29]

According to Zaspel New Covenant Theology is more of a movement than a recognized theology, but that is changing quickly. From Zaspel we learn another aspect of their view; there is no agreement on eschatology. As both Covenant Theology and Dispensationalism allow their covenant understanding to include eschatology I find it a little frustrating reading NCT authors where there seems to be purposeful avoidance of any eschatological

---

[29]   Fred G. Zaspel, A Brief Explanation of "New Covenant Theology," www.biblicalstudies

connections. This may be the result of its early development or as I suspect, it reveals a weakness in their system.

Are the creators of New Covenant Theology taking the best of both Covenant Theology and Dispensationalism and creating a hybrid theology or is this a clear and new way to understand how the Bible fits together? The jury is still out. As Zaspel said, NCT is a work in progress. The leaders of NCT are unhappy with dispensationalism and cannot endorse Covenant Theology (most Baptists get a little queasy about baptizing infants). Therefore, they desire to offer a third way, something beyond dispensationalism and Covenant Theology, and in so doing better reflect the teachings of the New Testament.

Zaspel continues to define New Covenant Theology:

NCT claims simply to have middle ground between these two. We are not satisfied with the simple "one covenant—two administrations" idea of Covenant Theology. In our judgment this results in a rather "flat" reading of Scripture which fails to appreciate the advance, the distinctively "new" character of this Messianic age. Nor are we satisfied with the over-compartmentalizing tendency of Dispensational Theology. In our judgment it's "no law" and "two equal peoples" notions failed to appreciate the unity of God's nature and purpose. And so we find ourselves somewhere between the two traditional answers. [30]

Zaspel explains the dilemma of many; not being able to accept traditional Covenant Theology nor dispensationalism. I agree the "two administrations" of Covenant Theology and the "two equal peoples" of dispensationalism are enough to reject both systems.

There are differences among authors of New Covenant Theology, especially the amount of Old Testament law which is allowed in the new covenant and the amount of grace we see under the old covenant.

---

[30] Ibid.

Zaspel sees a mixture of both yet stresses grace as the primary force under the new covenant:

NCT also recognizes that law and grace are sometimes names for the two periods covered by the Old and New Covenants, but we would look at the two words as also defining two emphases, not the replacement of law by grace. We would see a greater emphasis on grace under the New Covenant and generally a more legal character to the Old Covenant. In short, we would argue that law remains (contra Dispensational Theology), but with signification alteration (contra Covenant Theology). There are varying degrees of general agreement with this on all sides, of course, but these points of emphasis tend to distinguish NCT.[31]

Zaspel says the **"law remains"** but with **"alteration."** I suppose he means the Mosaic Law which seems to weaken the purpose for New Covenant Theology in the first place. Or is there another law he has in view? Here is a place where details of their theology must be clarified.

A common criticism from advocates of NCT is how Covenant Theology divides the Law of Moses into three sections; they allow part of the Law into the new covenant while disallowing other parts. I agree: this is a major flaw of not only Covenant theology but the thinking of many Christians.

A New Testament authority is needed before any old practices are imposed or required. That's because the Law of Moses, the old covenant, the Torah, is obsolete. We are not under that law; we are not obligated to keep laws that were given to the Israelites only.[32]

With this I find agreement. It is a matter of authority. Does the old covenant have authority once the new covenant is established? What is the source of that authority? Covenant Theology, I think, would argue it is the authority of God. The Law of Moses is the Law of God and therefore carries authority no matter the time frame. The

---

[31] Ibid.
[32] Grace Communion Internation-www.gci.org

new covenant is not all that "new" under Covenant Theology; it is another administration of grace, which happens to be in the same covenant as Moses and the Law of God.

Is the Mosaic Law in or out? If part of it is in, what hermeneutic is New Covenant Theology using to allow any part of the law in? Scripture points to the conclusion that either we practice all the law or we see all the law fulfilled in Christ. Again, New Covenant Theology makes strides in the right direction but seems hesitant about this final and important step.

No one can argue the Mosaic Law was in authority in the Old Testament. Yet, I would argue that its authority is temporary. Nevertheless, we are still are under the Law of God, which in the new covenant is the Law of Christ. The Law of Christ also carries the authority of God. It is not necessary to be under Moses to be under God's authority. If we are still under Moses, then accepting Christ as King and mediator of a new covenant is not relevant today.

New Covenant Theology sees a clear difference between what was fading away, the old covenant with its ten commandments, and what was replacing it, the glorious new covenant. This sharp break between the old and the new is a basic premise of New Covenant Theology.

John G. Reisinger, author of <u>New Covenant Theology and Prophecy</u>, asked four basic questions and they are excellent to use determining our position on covenant:

1. *Exactly what is the Old and what is the New Covenant?*
2. *Exactly what is the relationship of these two covenants to each other and to the rest of Scripture?*
3. *Specifically with whom were each of these two covenants made?*
4. *What is the exact status and function of each of these covenants today?*

When I answer these questions biblically, it becomes impossible for me to fit into either a Dispensational or a Covenant Theology camp.

I answer all four of these questions differently than both a Dispensationalist and a Covenant Theologian.[33]

As we progress towards a new way of understanding covenant, we can use some of the New Covenant Theology arguments as they will be similar as what I am saying. The reason in my mind why New Covenant Theology is a non-starter is based on three areas of difficulty:

1. Until their position is clear about what part of Mosaic Law—even with alteration—enters the new Covenant, I cannot support it.

2. Lack of appreciation of the Holy Spirit in the new covenant. Their views are not clearly stated but my guess would be most supporting New Covenant Theology also support cessationism. This will only slightly change the basic system of theology but will have HUGE impact on the application of the theology.

3. Their insistence that covenant and eschatology must be viewed separately. Although this may seem small since I agree on many points, yet it is paramount as to how one sees the ongoing work of the kingdom in the new covenant. Redemptive history includes God's plan for the last days (first century) and the coming of the kingdom; which takes us to the heart of eschatology, which New Covenant Theology does not include, in my opinion. They make major strides from Covenant Theology and Dispensationalism, but what is missing is just too important to skip over.

Who wins the second round? By my count Covenant Theology has an easy win over dispensationalism in the first round but going against New Covenant theology too many weakness were revealed

---

[33]   John G. Reisinger, What is New Covenant Theology?

and it lost badly. We move to our final match, 'New Covenant Theology' verses 'Better Covenant Theology.'

Three up and three down. What is left? We must return to our core beliefs and adjust our view concerning covenant to align with the central message of the Bible; the kingship of Jesus and his eternal reign. With this in view our path to a glorious and better covenant is not only attainable but will be a joyful journey.

Section Two –
The Glorious Covenant Is Better
Covenant Theology

Chapter 5

The Glorious Covenant is a New Covenant

After reviewing three options about covenant I am still searching for something better. We want covenant to flow with, not against our eschatology. We want covenant which clearly divides history; a time before Christ and then after Christ. He must be center to history and theology. I suggest we look for a new and better way to understand covenant in the Bible. We need a view which stays true to the message of the New Testament concerning a new creation. We need a view which embraces a present and advancing kingdom. We need a view which gives the Spirit his proper role in administering the covenant. We need a view that seriously considers a preterist outlook on New Testament prophecy. At this time we have no established theological position meeting these parameters.

We are at the beginning of this theological development. Once we have a broad outline of where we are heading, I believe more details will be filled in. Our understanding needs to catch up with what the Holy Spirit is showing us. If we cannot present a solid biblical presentation we will not be able to teach it. Truth must be taught in a manner so those taught become teachers. This was Paul's desire for Timothy (II Tim. 2:2). Our challenge is the same. First, we need a multitude of Bible teachers to lay out the broad outlines of the Better Covenant. Second, once we have the bulk of information pointing in a similar direction; we can work together to solidify and strengthen our position so as to show a united front to the church.

What is presented here is my attempt to push these concepts into open dialog.

In the next section we examine the new covenant using the term "Better Covenant Theology" (first coined by Dr. Jonathan Welton). We both agree the previous doctrines of covenant are insufficient and have led the church in wrong directions. I will focus on propositions which are necessary for a fresh approach to covenants. This is only a start; some points over time may need reworking to match our growing revelation. Other points may be eliminated; time will tell. What this does represent is an attempt to move the church away from past theologies and towards a better future.

Since eschatology and covenant are joined in a united vision of God's purpose, there are overlapping elements which I covered extensively in my book <u>Glorious Kingdom</u>. I will refrain from repeating as much as possible.

In their book <u>Kingdom through Covenant</u>, Peter Gentry and Stephen Wellum state several guidelines in building a fresh view on covenants. I find two are helpful in our ongoing discussions.

1. The significance of progressive revelation for the unfolding of the biblical covenants.

With every Old Testament covenant God increases the level of understanding of his ultimate purpose. We call this 'progressive revelation.' Even though we not analyzing the Old Testament covenants as individual covenants (Edenic, Noachian, Abrahamic, Mosaic, Davidic, and Jeremiah's New Covenant), we need to see how these move the people of God towards the ultimate goal; the new covenant. When we arrive in the first century and Christ establishes the new covenant by pouring his blood upon the heavenly altar, it is the conclusion and fulfillment of all previous covenants. Although as we will see, the Mosaic covenant is fulfilled in Christ, the Abraham and Davidic serve as covenants of promise, which functions differently than the Law of Moses.

2. The new covenant supersedes all previous covenants in redemptive-history.[34]

The new covenant instituted by Christ is the goal of all previous covenants. This is the 'Better Covenant' and will never be replaced, renewed or need any improvements. The promises—Messianic prophecies, the types and shadows, the symbolism, everything found in the Old Testament—have their end with the new covenant. We must not stir the new into a mixture of Old Testament covenants. It stands alone, high and superior, not only in its establishment (Jesus' work on the cross) but what it provides to the people of God.

After years of intense studies in eschatology, particularly the kingdom of God I now see covenant as the partner of purpose with kingdom. Therefore, I readily admit, I come to covenant with certain presuppositions. If any view violates my confirmed revelation of the kingdom I will continue my quest. My goal with covenant is to learn how the new covenant flows with the present kingdom of God and to see how their unity brings greater clarity to the church.

Since this is not a complete guide to all things covenantal, I will limit the subject matter to the theology of the old and new covenant. Yet, it is not 'theological' in the manner Covenant Theology was explained because I frame my position around two named covenants in Scripture; the old and the new covenant.

After reviewing three positions on covenant, which I find inadequate, we move forward searching for a better approach. I build my position around 11 propositions and conclude with practical considerations.

Our first step in building a new perspective of covenant is viewing the covenant established by Jesus as entirely new. It is called New to set it apart from other covenants. The New Testament portrays the old covenant as temporary, which means its "use by date" is approaching. Jesus the Messiah establishes the eternal covenant, the

---

[34] Peter J. Gentry, Stephen J. Wellum, Kingdom through Covenant, Crossway, Wheaton, Illinois, 2012, p. 602-604

new covenant, the covenant of peace and the better covenant. These are different terms for the one and same covenant; referred in the New Testament most often as the new covenant. Every promise in the Old Testament, all types and shadows, the covenants of Abraham and David, they all come to their fulfillment in Christ. When the newness of the new covenant is dulled we lose what it came to accomplish: to fulfill prior covenants and bring the renewed people of God into their calling. Under this better covenant we live in the realm of the Spirit and therefore, can walk in the purposes of God.

When Jeremiah spoke of a *new covenant* for a future people of God, he gave the reason why it is necessary; God said, "*My covenant that they broke.*" God reaffirms that the covenant was his idea. It was established to create, protect and use a people for his purposes. Israel broke the covenant. We cannot rush over this statement like it never mattered. A new covenant is needed because the old was violated and is no longer useful. Therefore any attempt to resuscitate the old or mix in the new is wrong from the beginning. The new covenant is **new**. We cannot overstate this.

Dispensationalism with its discontinuity plus postponement view fails to see the new covenant in light of the church. They turn the church into a subplot of God's purposes while He waits for the real plan—the fulfillment of Old Testament promises through natural Israel. So even though they speak of newness, it is not the newness of the covenant but of the creation of the church, which was a mystery prior to Jesus.

Covenant Theology with its stress on continuity overlooks the aspect of newness of the covenant instituted by Jesus. Therefore, too much of Old Testament law enters the age of the new covenant. They correctly see the church as fulfilling promises and prophecies of the old covenant but their failure to see how the new covenant is truly a new thing is a major failure in their interpretation.

New Covenant Theology is correct in stressing the newness of the new covenant. Its proponents see the Law of Christ as replacing the

Mosaic Law. They offer a fresh perspective which needs to be heard. As I said earlier, their failure is separating covenant from eschatology. Doing so creates an unbalanced view of the church and removes the church as the people directly involved in bringing about the renewal of the earth. It separates the church from the Kingdom.

The better covenant established by Jesus is exactly what the book of Hebrews states; it is new. It is superior to the old covenant in all areas. It cannot be compared to anything previous because it does what others never did; the redemption of humankind by inward transformation.

Hebrews 10:19-22

Therefore, brothers, since we have confidence to enter the holy places by the blood of Jesus, [20] by the new and living way that he opened for us through the curtain, that is, through his flesh, [21] and since we have a great priest over the house of God, [22] let us draw near with a true heart in full assurance of faith, with our hearts sprinkled clean from an evil conscience and our bodies washed with pure water.

"*The new and living way*" is what Christians follow. We are not followers of an old way. We must come to Jesus with "*full assurance of faith*" the new covenant has power to "*clean from an evil conscience.*" Jesus prepared a way for all peoples. He offered his blood in the heavenly altar and purchased eternal salvation. It cannot be overstated; Jesus opened a **new** way for people. It is not a continuation or renewal of the old; **it is NEW!**

The Law of Moses was but a shadow of what came in Jesus.

Adam Clarke comments on Hebrews 10:1:

"The law, having a shadow of good things to come"- A shadow, skia, signifies, 1. Literally, the shade cast from a body of any kind, interposed between the place on which the shadow is projected, and the sun or light; the rays of the light not shining on that place,

because intercepted by the opacity of the body, through which they cannot pass.

2. It signifies, technically, a sketch, rude plan, or imperfect draught of a building, landscape, man, beast, &c. 3. It signifies, metaphorically, any faint adumbration, symbolical expression, imperfect or obscure image of a thing... The law, with all its ceremonies and sacrifices, was only a shadow of spiritual and eternal good. The Gospel is the image or thing itself, as including every spiritual and eternal good.[35]

Clarke's commentary is not easy to follow but his words concerning the law open up a better appreciation of why it needs to be replaced. Clarke speaks of the Mosaic Law as, "imperfect or obscure image of a thing" and "vain, empty." He says that the Law as a shadow was a "sketch" or a "rude place" or an imperfect drawing of a building. The Law is not the final perfect establishment of God's moral standard for the ages. It was only the shadow of the eternal plan of God brought about with the coming of Jesus. It was given to one nation, a people living in a specific land for a certain time period and for that purpose is worked well.

Clarke continues with his comments on verse 19:

Boldness to enter, Liberty, full access to the entrance of the holy place. This is an allusion to the case of the high priest going into the holy of holies. He went with fear and trembling, because, if he had neglected the smallest item prescribed by the law, he could expect nothing but death. Genuine believers can come even to the throne of God with confidence, as they carry into the Divine presence the infinitely meritorious blood of the great atonement; and, being justified through that blood, they have a right to all the blessings of the eternal kingdom.[36]

---

[35] Adam Clarke, Adam Clarke's Commentary on the Bible, Nelson Reference; abridged edition 1997)

[36] Ibid.

When Jesus offered his blood for the atonement of humankind it opened for all "the blessings of the eternal kingdom." I like that.

The new covenant is perfect; the old covenant was not! The new covenant is new. It replaced the old. As simple as this is, it amazes me how the church has found ways to muddle its clear intentions. In Jesus we are a new creation (II Cor. 5:17). The old creation (old covenant) is now gone and never will return.

Chapter 6

The Glorious Covenant Unites
the People of God

The new covenant creates a new humanity. This radical concept shook the first century, both religious and civil society. From the Jewish perspective, humanity was divided into two groups; Jews and Gentiles. The Romans had their divisions, so did the Greeks, and so forth. Certain things were common throughout the known world; slaves and women were at the bottom of societal order. In the new covenant how will God structure his people? The story of Israel for centuries reinforced the concept, "We are the people of God," everybody else is outside looking in. When the new covenant is established God widens the borders and brings in peoples from all nations, races and traditions. Out of all peoples God creates his new eschatological family. This is a new and unique family where there is *"neither Jew nor Greek, there is neither slave nor free, there is no male and female, for you are all one in Christ Jesus* (Gal. 3:28).

Biblical scholars have debated and gone back and forth concerning whether Paul taught the concept of a third race. Race as we understand it is not the best word, yet for the Jews it was simple. Jews were God's people and all other ethnicities were Gentiles. Even though in the first century this co-called Gentile 'race' was divided into numerous races (African, Asian, Indian, Etc.) and many lived a great distance from the first century Mediterranean world.

What this brings into focus is the church of the Messiah, those baptized into his body, are not thought of as being Jew nor Gentile, but as a third people group; a holy people according to Peter.

I Peter 2:9

But you are a chosen race, a royal priesthood, a holy nation, a people for his own possession, that you may proclaim the excellencies of him who called you out of darkness into his marvelous light.

Two-thousand years ago it was unthinkable for anyone to suggest traditional definitions could be abolished. But that was the Christian message! God was in Christ reconciling all people through faith into a new family. Paul makes this clear in his letter to the Ephesians.

Ephesians 2:11-16

Therefore remember that at one time you Gentiles in the flesh, called "the uncircumcision" by what is called the circumcision, which is made in the flesh by hands— [12] remember that you were at that time separated from Christ, alienated from the Commonwealth of Israel and strangers to the covenants of promise, having no hope and without God in the world. [13] But now in Christ Jesus you who once were far off have been brought near by the blood of Christ. [14] For he himself is our peace, who has made us both one and has broken down in his flesh the dividing wall of hostility [15] by abolishing the law of commandments expressed in ordinances, that he might create in himself one new man in place of the two, so making peace, [16] and might reconcile us both to God in one body through the cross, thereby killing the hostility.

Paul writes about Gentiles who are *"in Christ"* are now included in the *"Commonwealth of Israel."* In Christ both Jew and Gentile are one. All divisions are broken down, none are left. Through the cross of Jesus God creates a new humanity; one *"new man"* in place of two. This is dispensationalists' major flaw, refusing to accept there is but one people of God. Gentiles before the coming of Jesus were *"strangers to the covenants of promise."* What covenants does Apostle Paul refer to? The Mosaic Covenant is not a "covenant of promise." Israel was not waiting centuries for a renewal of Mosaic Law. The covenants of promise were given to Abraham and David. Those in Christ are now "brought near" to these covenants and included in the promises.

The *"Commonwealth of Israel"* is what we may call citizenship. When part of the commonwealth a person has all the privileges and blessing common to all. Being part of the commonwealth means you are not a second class citizen. This is the essence what Paul is saying. Once Gentiles are saved and *"in Christ"* then there remains no division between Jews and Christians. Yet this brings up a crucial point where many fail to understand. Do saved Gentiles join the ethnic nation of Israel? Is the whole of first century Israel automatically included? Paul addresses this in his letter to the Romans.

Has Israel Been Rejected?

From dispensationalists we hear cries of "Replacement Theology!" "Replacement Theology!" They are expecting people of other views to run and hide when these threatening words are spoken. What did Apostle Paul say about this subject? Did he believe in the continuity of Israel or is he on the side of discontinuity? Did he teach replacement or natural fulfillment or spiritual fulfillment? Does Paul embrace the doctrine of two peoples of God (Israel and the Church)?

Romans 11:1

I ask, then, has God rejected his people? By no means!

Dispensationalists often quote this question and answer from Paul. It is straight-forward; God has not rejected the Jews. But Paul does not stop here and move to another subject. He explains WHY he is confident God still works with the Jews.

For I myself am an Israelite, a descendant of Abraham, a member of the tribe of Benjamin.

What is Paul's argument? "I am a Jew and I have not been rejected!" If even one Jew embraces the Messiah, then how can we say, "God has rejected his people?" The book of Acts shows the early church for a number of years was exclusively Jewish. Paul reminds his readers of Elijah and uses his story as an example of what is taking place now.

Romans 11:3-5

God has not rejected his people whom he foreknew. Do you not know what the Scripture says of Elijah, how he appeals to God against Israel? [3]"Lord, they have killed your prophets, they have demolished your altars, and I alone am left, and they seek my life." [4]But what is God's reply to him? "I have kept for myself seven thousand men who have not bowed the knee to Baal." [5]So too at the present time there is a remnant, chosen by grace.

God has more followers than we know. He has a remnant. Paul is part of this Jewish remnant. As a nation, the majority of Jews came under judgment, just as John the Baptist foretold (Matt. 3:7-10). Yet, a remnant of Jews became the first fruits of the new covenant.

So when the argument "God never rejected his people" is put forward, it must be placed in Paul's context. The majority of the nation WAS rejected, but a remnant was saved. The rejection was based upon their own decision in refusing Jesus as Israel's Messiah. John 1:11 states this, *"He came to his own and his own people did not receive him."*

Reading down the chapter in Romans we encounter a statement which is overlooked. People love to quote verse one and stop; but continue to read.

Romans 11:13-15

Now I am speaking to you Gentiles. Inasmuch then as I am an apostle to the Gentiles, I magnify my ministry [14] in order somehow to make my fellow Jews jealous, **and thus save**

some of them. [15] For if **their rejection** means the reconciliation of the world, what will their acceptance mean but life from the dead?

Paul is not schizophrenic; his argument is sound, that is, if we read it in context. He is adamant *"God has not rejected his people* (vs.1)*"* and then later he writes *"their rejection"* will bring about the salvation of the world. What is going on Paul? Who is being rejected? And who is being saved? And how does all this relate to the world being saved?

First, the first fruits of Israel are the remnant. The first apostles, the early followers of Jesus and the church at Pentecost, all belong to this group. They accepted their Messiah. They made the transition from the old to the new covenant. They are not rejected, even though Israel as a covenant-breaking nation was rejected. But it is not all bad news, because God turns the bad choice of Israel in the good news for the world. The rejection (Israel having the kingdom taken away, Matt. 21:43) results in a saved remnant and these first fruits people (the harvest of believing Jews) open the door for Gentiles being added, and therefore, the *"reconciliation of the world."*

Yes, I agree, Paul could have explained it better for those of us living almost 2,000 years later. Nevertheless, if read in context, withholding our preconceived doctrines, it can be understood.

Romans 9:1-3

I am speaking the truth in Christ—I am not lying; my conscience bears me witness in the Holy Spirit— [2] that I have great sorrow and unceasing anguish in my heart. [3] For I could wish that I myself were accursed and cut off from Christ for the sake of my brothers, my kinsmen according to the flesh.

Why is Paul willing to be accursed if the natural descendants of Abraham-Israel were fine as they were? If we see modern Israel as God's chosen people then certainly the Jews of the first century would be the same? Paul was concerned for his *"kinsmen according to the flesh.*" He knew the decision to move out of the old covenant into the new was difficult because of their stubbornness of heart and unwillingness to believe Jesus. Nevertheless, he writes a simple guideline for viewing Israel after the flesh.

Romans 9:4-5

They are Israelites, and to them belong the adoption, the glory, the covenants, the giving of the law, the worship, and the promises. ⁵ To them belong the patriarchs, and from their race, according to the flesh, is the Christ, who is God over all, blessed forever. Amen.

Paul honors natural Israel for their place in salvation history. They were the only people, the only nation, receiving God's covenants and experiencing his glory. And the highest honor they have is being the people bringing forth God's Messiah, the Christ.

If the kingdom is taken away from Israel and given to another nation (Matt.21:43) and if their temple is to be left desolate (Matt. 23:38) and they are under a soon coming judgment, then, has the word of God failed? Paul's words to those living in Thessalonica sounds like all is lost.

I Thessalonians 2:14-16

For you, brothers, became imitators of the churches of God in Christ Jesus that are in Judea. For you suffered the same things from your own countrymen as they did from the Jews, ¹⁵ who killed both the Lord Jesus and the prophets, and drove us out, and displease God and oppose all mankind ¹⁶ by hindering us from speaking to the Gentiles that they might be saved—so as always to fill up the measure of their sins. But wrath has come upon them at last!

God's wrath is about to be poured out on the Jews. Their sin has now come to the full. The final sin is refusing their Messiah and having him put to death. This being true, how does Paul answer his own question concerning the faithfulness of God's word?

Romans 9:6-8

But it is not as though the word of God has failed. For not all who are descended from Israel belong to Israel, [7] and not all are children of Abraham because they are his offspring, but "Through Isaac shall your offspring be named." [8] This means that it is not the children of the flesh who are the children of God, but the children of the promise are counted as offspring.

These words of Paul are critical to understanding what is taking place in the new covenant. The Prophets are filled with promises for Israel in the future (the last days or as Daniel says, the time of the end). Will God then, because of Israel's unbelief, fail in fulfilling his word? No, says Paul. The reason, because Israel is a mixed nation, not all *belong to Israel.* The true children of Israel were always people of faith. The children born of the flesh are not automatically included; only those of faith are part of the people of God receiving the promises.

As Paul continues his argument he builds his remnant theology.

Romans 9:27 & 30-33

And Isaiah cries out concerning Israel: "Though the number of the sons of Israel be as the sand of the sea, only a remnant of them will be saved.

[30] What shall we say, then? That Gentiles who did not pursue righteousness have attained it, that is, a righteousness that is by faith; [31] but that Israel who pursued a law that would lead to righteousness did not succeed in reaching that law. [32] Why? Because they did not pursue it by faith, but as if it were based on works. They have stumbled over the stumbling stone, [33] as it is written, "Behold, I am laying in Zion a stone of stumbling, and a

rock of offense; and whoever believes in him will not be put to shame."

Paul uses the words of Isaiah to back up his point. *"Only a remnant of them will be saved,"* because Israel did not pursue their calling in faith. Israel rejected their Christ and he became their *"stone of stumbling."*

Romans 10:1-4

Brothers, my heart's desire and prayer to God for them is that they may be saved. [2] For I bear them witness that they have a zeal for God, but not according to knowledge. [3] For, being ignorant of the righteousness of God, and seeking to establish their own, they did not submit to God's righteousness. [4] For Christ is the end of the law for righteousness to everyone who believes.

Israel possessed a zeal for God but without knowledge. Paul says they are ignorant of the "righteousness of God." What righteousness are they ignorant of? Certainly not the Law of Moses?

Israel refused the righteousness of God which was revealed through their Messiah, Jesus. By sending Jesus, Yahweh was being righteous and demonstrating his commitment to the promises he made to Israel. Paul said Israel did not submit to God's righteousness. Again, they had no problem with the Law of Moses; it was Jesus who gave them fits. It was Jesus they refused to submit to. He was proof of the righteousness of God. God never forgets his promises. He is a God of covenant.

Isaiah and the New Covenant

Several Old Testament promises dealt with the future covenant and the Messiah/servant who would inaugurate it. We are familiar with Jeremiah's prophecy so here are passages from Isaiah about how Israel's God would do a new thing.

I will keep you and give you as a **covenant** to the people (Is. 49:8).

For the mountains may depart and the hills removed, but my steadfast love shall not depart from you and my **covenant of peace** shall not be removed (Is. 54:10).

I will make with you and **everlasting covenant**, my steadfast, sure love for David (Is. 55:3).

And a Redeemer will come to Zion, to those in Jacob who turn from transgression, declares the Lord. And as for me, this is **my covenant** with them, says the Lord: My Spirit that is upon you, and my words that I have put in your mouth shall not depart out of your mouth, or out of the mouth of your offspring, or out of the mouth of your children's offspring, says the Lord, from this time and forever more. (Is. 59:20-21).

I will make an **everlasting covenant** with them, their offspring shall be known among the nations (Is. 61:8).

Beginning in Isaiah forty-nine and continuing to the end of the chapter, new life springing from an everlasting covenant is portrayed in vivid language. These different phrases, "Covenant," "Covenant of Peace," and "Everlasting Covenant," all refer to a single covenant; the new covenant which arrives with Jesus. Although we give Jeremiah credit as the first to prophesy the new covenant, Isaiah had it in view 200 years earlier.

Several conditions and blessings are associated with the coming covenant. First, the covenant establishes peace. Second, the covenant people will have the Spirit. Third, these "offspring" will be known among the nations. This means they are a people of influence. Putting this together we get a picture of God's restored people through Jesus. A people of the Holy Spirit experiencing peace and passing it on to generation after generation. Is the church today a place of peace? Are we ministering peace to those around us?

Isaiah 32:17

And the effect of righteousness will be peace, and the result of righteousness, quietness and trust forever.

There is no need to sermonize, the word is clear. True righteousness which is found through Christ in the new covenant brings peace. God help us realize we are the one new people of God, the Church of Jesus, and let it be known throughout the world as a place of peace.

Chapter 7

Glorious Covenant is Life in the Spirit

If we can point to one element which distinguishes the old covenant from the new, it is the role of the Holy Spirit. The old was based upon law and strict obedience to an objective standard. The Spirit is not absent in the Old Testament but only a few received his power. The new is entirely different. Every member of Christ's body is indwelt by the Spirit of God. Paul wrote the old covenant was a ministry of death whereas the new produces life (II Cor.3:6). One covenant is temporary in nature and the other is eternal.

The Pentecostal movement (1906) and the Charismatic movement (1960s) failed in producing many biblical scholars. Theirs was a movement of experience. Establishing this personal and corporate touch from the Spirit was important because by the end of the 20th century Evangelicalism was adrift toward coldness, lack of passion and doctrinal squabbling. The wind of the Spirit brought revival around the world.

With over one hundred years of Pentecostalism, we learned more than a few things. One, and possibly the most important, unless there are regular outpourings of the Spirit, the church grows cold, legalistic, and denominational. Over the past decades we have seen a number of outpourings and revivals and those receiving each wave move forward in the purposes of God. A sad part of history is when a new flow of the Spirit comes upon a people, those pioneers of the previous movement of the Spirit are among the first to reject it. It is scary how fast a church or movement can move from pioneering a present move of God to being passé and out of touch. One of the reasons for this spiritual backsliding is lack of progress in biblical revelation. When we stop learning we begin falling behind.

When there are heightened experiences with the Holy Spirit and the church comes alive with God's presence and power, it opens the door for fresh revelation. We are currently seeing a revival within Spirit-filled movements where hunger for the word matches their excitement in the Spirit. Present truth and experience have finally met. Both must be kept in balance. The Holy Spirit is bringing us into waves of biblical revelation not just spiritual experiences, or better put, emotional experiences. Some of my greatest spiritual experiences have been through revelation of the Spirit in the word of God. One wave contains the seeds of the next wave. This means, now is a great time to connect to the local church. It is time to connect with those riding the wave and not run to the shore. The wave of kingdom understanding contains the seed of covenant understanding.

Charismatics are starting to take the biblical text seriously. One area these Spirit-filled people should be able to write about with confidence is the role of the Holy Spirit as it pertains to the new covenant. We have many books on the filling and gifts of the Spirit but few on Spirit and covenant.

New Covenant Obedience

In the Old Testament, Torah (Mosaic Law) was the objective standard of written laws. It was to be observed by Israel to insure God's blessings. Digging into the human condition even slightly reveals we have an inclination towards rules. We like being told what to do. It makes life simpler. Responsibility then is placed on someone else. Of, course in any society, there is need for order, or complete chaos would result. Yet, we must not carry this natural yearning for rules into the new covenant. Why? If we only learn how to walk in rules we never learn how to walk in the Spirit. We are required to grow up. We are placed in a covenant where walking by the Spirit is not an option.

Under the new covenant, we have no official list of laws. If you take time to make a list, you will find over 1,000 commandments. Yet, we never find any admonition or instructions to create a formal list of rules. The church will make a serious error if we replace 613 Mosaic laws for over 1,000 New Testament laws. Are we to ignore the many commandments in the New Testament? As Paul would say, by no means! Yet, here is the dilemma: when we attempt to obey New Testament laws with the same diligence as Old Testament believers, we find ourselves in stress because they are difficult to keep. New Testament laws are more difficult to keep than even the Laws of Moses. The harder we try, the guiltier we feel. We need a different approach.

The Holy Spirit is the difference. Only by being filled and led by the Spirit of God can we fulfill what is expected of us.

Galatians 5:16-18:

But I say, walk by the Spirit, and you will not gratify the desires of the flesh. [17] For the desires of the flesh are against the Spirit, and the desires of the Spirit are against the flesh, for these are opposed to each other, to keep you from doing the things you want to do. [18] But if you are led by the Spirit, you are not under the law.

This passage, for the most part, is used by preachers to show how Christians battle the flesh. We hear sermons on our evil flesh and how close we are to falling off the cliff into an abyss of sin. We are told of the daily battle between the flesh and the Spirit, with little hope of victory. Yes, Paul sees the flesh and Spirit in opposition, but what is the context?

Beginning in chapter one Paul is concerned that the Galatians are turning to a different gospel (1:6). In chapter two Paul confronts Peter in his hypocrisy concerning keeping the Law (2:11-14). In chapter three Paul asks the pertinent question, *"Did you receive the Spirit by works of the Law or by hearing with faith (3:2)?"* The whole of chapter three is the debate between law and grace. In verse 13 he boldly states, *"Christ redeemed us from the curse of the law (3:13)."* Read chapter four, the same subject. Why then when we get to verses in 5:16-18 we turn away from the context and make it about our personal spiritual warfare? I believe Paul does not depart from his subject, but frames his next argument around the 'flesh' and 'Spirit.' He is still teaching us about the "Law" and how Christians are no longer subject to its binding authority.

Pastor, Bible scholar, and author Joe McIntyre:

"A good case could be made for Paul's concept of the flesh as a realm in which we formerly lived and in that realm the Jews lived under law. But the dawning of the Messianic age has brought us into the Spirit/spirit realm. In Galatians Paul assigns the law to the present age and in 1:4 he says Christ has delivered us out of the present age. To be "in the Spirit/spirit" is to be in the age to come which has arrived in Christ's resurrection."[37]

Gordon D. Fee is acclaimed among the top New Testament scholars in the world. His excellent book, God's Empowering Presence, is a gift to the church for generations to come. What is the meaning of "flesh" or at least how does Paul use it? Fee explains: in the Old Testament it primarily refers to the "flesh of the bodies" and, *"few occasions the term is extended to describe human frailty and creatureliness... It would be unthinkable to the Hebrew that sin lay in the flesh, since sin's origins lie in the human heart".[38]*

Fee: *"Although Paul rarely uses flesh in its basic sense, as referring to the physical body, he regularly uses it the extended sense as referring to our humanity in some way or another... Paul recognizes present human life as still "in the flesh" (Gal. 2:20, 2 Cor. 10:3), not at all intending a morally pejorative sense to the word."[39]*

Fee suggests we come to a passage like Galatians 5:16 without automatically making "flesh" equivalent to our "sinful nature." Should we interpret Paul's "flesh" as anthropological or eschatological? If we see in the first sense we then ascribe "sinful

---

[37]   Joe McIntyre, From a personal E-Mail, 2014
[38]   Gordon D. Fee, God's Empowering Presence, Hendrickson Publishers, 1994, p.815
[39]   Ibid.

nature" to it, yet, if we ascribe the latter we see it in a wider context of Mosaic Law versus the new covenant. Fee takes considerable space in his book showing how the text (Gal.5:16-18) and the context (book of Galatians and the whole of Scripture) point to eschatology with the frailty of human flesh as secondary in Paul's thinking.[40]

If Fee is correct, then, Paul is not setting up a structure where Christians are in continuous warfare against their flesh. For Paul the life in the Spirit is moving beyond law keeping, which belongs to the past.

Fee: *"Nowhere does Paul describe life in the Spirit as one of constant struggle with the flesh...Thus for Paul the language 'according to the flesh' describes both the perspective and the behavior of the former age that is passing away: those who so live will not inherit the kingdom of God (Gal.5:21)".[41]*

Fee: *"For Paul the Spirit marks the effective end of Torah, both because the coming of the Spirit fulfills the eschatological promise and signals the beginning of the new covenant."[42]*

When the day of Pentecost occurred, a variety of exciting things took place. Joel's prophecy is being fulfilled, people are speaking languages they never learned, a mass conversion of Jews takes place, yet, maybe the most important element is forgotten and Fee reminds us; the Mosaic age is finished and the age of the Spirit is upon us.

With this in mind Galatians 5 comes alive. It is more than Paul's admonition to live holy and keep the rules; it has as its backdrop old covenant manner of living (flesh). Therefore, if we live according to the flesh (keeping the old law), is living like we were in the older

---

[40] Gordon D. Fee, God's Empowering Presence, Hendrickson Publishers, 1994, p. 427-438, 803-826

[41] Ibid.

[42] Ibid.

age, the age of law. Paul says, "Walk in the Spirit" which is to live in the blessings of the new covenant.

By placing these verses within the larger context we have another example how eschatology and covenant are linked. The ending of Torah and the giving of the Spirit are eschatologically coupled. The new age of the Spirit, according to Paul, coincides with the ending of Mosaic Law. You cannot live according to the flesh (keeping commandments of the Law) and at the same time walk in the Spirit (living in the new covenant).

Paul ends with his long list of sins and fruit of the Spirit. Here, he contrasts people outside Christ and those in Christ walking according to the Spirit. I agree with Fee when he does not see this list as a standard separating good and bad Christians. Although Christians can and do fall into such vices, the point is the stark difference between those without faith and those with faith (of the new covenant).

Paul's point can also be seen in his understanding on how Gentiles are included in God's family.

Fee: *"The emphasis now, however, is not so much on Gentile inclusion per se, but on their inclusion totally apart from the Torah, which served as the "identity marker" of the former covenant, The Spirit, and **the Spirit alone**, Paul argues in Galatians, **identifies the people of God under the new covenant**.* "[43]

During the early days of the church, it finally dawned upon the Jewish believers, God is granting Gentiles salvation and admittance to his family. What was shocking—and extremely radical—was how this work of God was done: apart from the Law of Moses.

Fee makes a simple and profound conclusion:

---

[43]   Ibid.

"The promised new covenant has replaced the old, and the gift of the Spirit proves it."[44]

Day of Pentecost

One area of agreement with dispensationalism (there are not many) is the beginning of the church at Pentecost. Yes, the people of the Old Testament were gathered or assembled but the church of the new covenant was not complete until the Holy Spirit was poured out. Once Jesus ascended and was enthroned as King of all creation, and given dominion, a kingdom and glory, his first edict was to send the Holy Spirit.

John 16:7

Nevertheless, I tell you the truth: it is to your advantage that I go away, for if I do not go away, the Helper will not come to you. But if I go, I will send him to you.

Jesus before his Ascension gave the same promise:

Luke 24:49

And behold, I am sending the promise of my Father upon you. But stay in the city until you are clothed with power from on high.

The arrival of the Spirit is the *"Promise of the Father."* When this promise is received, the disciples will receive power from heaven; from the newly crowned King.

The coming of the Holy Spirit was predicted by the Old Testament Prophets.

Joel 2:28-29

And it shall come to pass afterward, that I will pour out my Spirit on all flesh; your sons and your daughters shall prophesy, your old men shall dream dreams, and your

---

[44]   Ibid.

young men shall see visions. Even on the male and female servants in those days I will pour out my Spirit.

Isaiah 32:15-16

Until the Spirit is poured upon us from on high, and the wilderness becomes a fruitful field, and the fruitful field is deemed a forest. Then justice will dwell in the wilderness, and righteousness abide in the fruitful field.

Isaiah 44: 3

For I will pour water on the thirsty land, and streams on the dry ground; I will pour my Spirit upon your offspring, and my blessing on your descendants.

Ezekiel 11:19

And I will give them one heart, and a new spirit I will put within them. I will remove the heart of stone from their flesh and give them a heart of flesh.

Ezekiel 36:27

And I will put my Spirit within you, and cause you to walk in my statutes and be careful to obey my rules.

Ezekiel 39:29

And I will not hide my face anymore from them, when I pour out my Spirit upon the house of Israel, declares the Lord GOD.

Volumes can be written on how the ministry of the Spirit is absolutely vital to the new covenant. Hopefully soon a book will be written on Covenant and Spirit. It will be written by a person committed to the present reality of the kingdom and the Spirit's power and gifts. The majority of scholarly works, including those on the Holy Spirit, are written by those denying a large portion's of the Spirit's present activity (cessationism).

This much we can say: along with the promise of a new covenant there are a variety of verses promising the gift of the Spirit in the new covenant age. When Pentecost came and Holy Spirit was poured out, the apostles knew it fulfilled what Jesus told them. They were told to wait, and in their waiting they received the power to function as ministers of the new covenant. Can we imagine the book of Acts without miracles? Yet, there are those in the church today attempting to function after stripping away the Spirit's power from God's people.

So much more needs to be said on the role of the Holy Spirit as connected with the new covenant. His role is vital in its initial inauguration and continuing administration. We need the Spirit. Without the filling of the Spirit we drift quickly back into the spirit of the old age, making and following laws. And then, this results in appearing to be religious but with little inner transformation. One thing is certain: Better Covenant Theology is committed to a central role for the Holy Spirit in our understanding and application of the new covenant.

Come, Holy Spirit!

Chapter 8

The Glorious Covenant Ends
the Mosaic Covenant

A majority of Old Testament scholars, both Christian and Jewish, agree there are 613 laws. Each and every law was to be kept by those following the Mosaic Covenant. It was a package deal. Even though advocates of Covenant Theology break the Mosaic Law into three divisions; the civil, the ceremonial and the moral, no such stated division is found in Scripture. When the New Testament refers to the Law; it means all 613.

For those not familiar with the Mosaic Law, all 613 laws of the old covenant, I have taken the space to list them, yes, all of them (see Appendix 1 at the back of the book). Most Christians hear about "The Law" but rarely take time to read the comprehensive list. We know the 10 commandments, laws about temple worship and food, but there are hundreds of Mosaic Laws we know little about. Therefore, I included them. I doubt if any will read all 613 in one setting, but maybe read 50 at a time. This is important because to fully appreciate our freedom in the new covenant we must have a grasp what we are freed from. Read them and see how life would be if our commitment to Christ was based upon our obedience to these laws.

How does the Mosaic Covenant relate to Christians today? How does the new covenant deal with the numerous laws of Moses? Must we keep all of them, some of them? In what way are they useful?

One argument from Apostle Paul is Christians are dead to the Law. What does this mean? For Paul the law is dead. *"For through the law I died to the law, so that I might live to God."* We may ask, is Paul's dying to the law the same as the law is dead. If as a Christian we are dead in relationship to the Mosaic Law, it then has no authority over us. For Christians the law is dead! It no longer has legal authority over us.

Anticipating questions on this matter Paul gives a simple example on the law of marriage. When a woman marries, Paul says, she is bound to her husband as long as he lives. If the husband dies, then the Law of marriage is no longer in effect, she is free to remarry (Rom. 7:1-3). Paul then writes:

Romans 7:4

Likewise, my brothers, you also have died to the law through the body of Christ, so that you may belong to another, to him who has been raised from the dead, in order that we may bear fruit for God.

When Jesus died upon the cross we died also. We died in our relationship to the Mosaic Law. Now we are married to another, the one who God raised from the dead, so we can bear fruit to God.

Romans 6:14

For sin will have no dominion over you, since you are not under law but under grace.

Paul is answering objections to his position on the Law. If we are not under the Law of Moses, then, why not sin? Experiencing grace is the path to living in dominion over sin. We are under the authority of grace and under the leadership of the Spirit. The Holy Spirit guides us into grace and we are under the authority of the new covenant.

I agree with Gentry and Wellum that the old covenant is a package covenant.

"In the Old Testament, the amount of space devoted to the 'old covenant' is vast, yet Scripture teaches that it is not an end in itself but rather a means to a larger end which culminates in a greater and better new covenant. This is why Scripture views the 'old covenant' as temporary in God's plan, or better, as a crucial part if

God's redemptive purposes, yet when that to which it points arrives, the covenant with Israel as a whole covenant package comes to its end and Christians are no longer under it as a covenant. "[45]

First, we will read the six occasions where the term "Law of Moses" is found in the New Testament.

Luke 2:22

And when the time came for their purification according to the Law of Moses, they brought him up to Jerusalem to present him to the Lord.

To understand the message of the gospels (Matthew, Mark, Luke and John) it is helpful to know that Jesus was born under the Mosaic Law and his father and mother raised him in like fashion. Here we see them following the laws of purification.

Luke 24:44-45

Then he said to them, "These are my words that I spoke to you while I was still with you, that everything written about me in the Law of Moses and the Prophets and the Psalms must be fulfilled." [45] Then he opened their minds to understand the Scriptures.

Luke records a noteworthy truth. Jesus states the Law of Moses, the Prophets, and the Psalms—the whole of the Old Testament Scriptures—was written with him in view. Not only does the Old Testament point to Jesus in types, shadows, prophecy, but in Jesus the Messiah everything is fulfilled. If all is fulfilled in Jesus, why do we look elsewhere to find fulfillments? It took Jesus opening their minds to *"understand the Scriptures;"* under the new covenant John says of the Holy Spirit, ***"he will guide you into all the truth (John 15:13).***

---

[45]   Peter J. Gentry, Stephen J. Wellum, Kingdom through Covenant, Crossway, Wheaton, Illinois, 2012, p. 635

John 7:23

If on the Sabbath a man receives circumcision, so that the Law of Moses may not be broken, are you angry with me because on the Sabbath I made a man's whole body well?

A point of contention Jewish leaders had with Jesus was his inconsistency in obeying Mosaic Laws. Jesus more than once points to the moral of the Law for which it was written. There is a higher law which fulfills the letter of the law.

Acts 28:23

When they had appointed a day for him, they came to him at his lodging in greater numbers. From morning till evening he expounded to them, testifying to the kingdom of God and trying to convince them about Jesus both from the Law of Moses and from the Prophets.

What was Paul's primary message? It was the kingdom of God, established through the death and resurrection of Jesus. What authority does Paul rely on? He teaches Jesus and his kingdom from the Old Testament. The reason we read and study the Scriptures in the Old Testament is more than revisiting history but to see Jesus and his kingdom.

1 Corinthians 9:9-12

For it is written in the Law of Moses, "You shall not muzzle an ox when it treads out the grain." Is it for oxen that God is concerned? [10] Does he not certainly speak for our sake? It was written for our sake, because the plowman should plow in hope and the thresher thresh in hope of sharing in the crop. [11] If we have sown spiritual things among you, is it too much if we reap material things from you? [12] If others share this rightful claim on you, do not we even more?

Paul uses one of the Laws of Moses as a background to show how ministers of the word of God, or ministers of the new covenant, have the right to be financially supported. Those who give their life to teaching others the word of God and sow spiritual things into the church have every right to be supported. Paul does not say the exact Law is binding, since it speaks of oxen, but uses the principle and applies the spiritual law.

Using the Law of Moses as foundation for new covenant teaching is not uncommon in the New Testament and we can learn hermeneutical lessons. We are not under Law but under Grace, therefore, we must learn to hear what the Holy Spirit is saying through the Law to Christian believers. This can only be done by thoroughly studying how the Jesus and his apostles interpreted Old Testament passages.

Hebrews 10:28

Anyone who has set aside the Law of Moses dies without mercy on the evidence of two or three witnesses.

If we only read verse twenty-eight we may be fearful of not keeping the Law of Moses. Please read on. The following verse compares those who *"set aside the law of Moses"* under the old covenant to those who *"profaned the blood of the covenant"* (new) and *"outraged the Spirit of Grace."* It does not say those under the new covenant must keep the Mosaic Law or be judged; it is a warning to those first century Jews who after professing Jesus and Messiah and then revert back to Judaism. *"How much worse punishment, do you think, will be deserved by the one who has trampled underfoot the Son of God, and has profaned the blood of the covenant by which he was sanctified, and has outraged the Spirit of grace (vs.29)?"*

The subject of the Law of Moses is not a small one; therefore it is easier to view particular aspects of the discussion by themselves.

Should Christians keep Jewish holidays? What about other laws? For us who treat holidays as an additional day off work this discussion may seem mute; but for Apostle Paul it was a serious matter. The first few years of the early church there was a common agreement to keep the Law of God. Why not? They were Jews and this is what Jews do. Once Gentiles turn to the Lord, the issue was brought before the Apostles and Elders. The verdict in Acts 15 let believing Gentiles off the hook of Moses; yet, it was still accepted that Christian Jews were still Jews and must keep the law. After a few years Apostle Paul lays out the theological groundwork of what Jesus accomplished in his death, resurrection and ascension. These Christ events changed everything. It took time, and it was not until the Romans destroyed the temple that the issue became settled. What is the final conclusion? Even believing Jews are not bound to the Mosaic code.

Colossians 2:16-17

> Therefore let no one pass judgment on you in questions of food and drink, or with regard to a festival or a new moon or a Sabbath. [17] These are a shadow of the things to come, but the substance belongs to Christ.

Paul was concerned about new covenant Christians submitting to Jewish laws. These laws were only the shadow of the things to come, which is Christ. We cannot stop people from judging us, but we can refuse to accept their opinion as valid. As we read Paul and his letters one concept is repeated; do not get entangled in Jewish laws.

In the first chapter of Galatians Paul is concerned about those who are *"quickly deserting"* Christ and *"turning to a different gospel."* This is serious. Paul exhorts the Galatians that even if an *"angel from heaven"* preaches a different gospel *"let him be accursed."* What is this different gospel? First, Paul said his gospel is not of man but a *"revelation of Jesus Christ."* As Paul continues the letter his perspective of this 'different gospel' is clarified.

Paul explains how he confronted Peter about his hypocrisy. What did Peter do wrong? Here is Paul's explanation.

Galatians 2:11-14

> "But when Cephas came to Antioch, I opposed him to his face, because he stood condemned. [12] For before certain

men came from James, he was eating with the Gentiles; but when they came he drew back and separated himself, fearing the circumcision party. [13] And the rest of the Jews acted hypocritically along with him, so that even Barnabas was led astray by their hypocrisy. [14] But when I saw that their conduct was not in step with the truth of the gospel, I said to Cephas before them all, "If you, though a Jew, live like a Gentile and not like a Jew, how can you force the Gentiles to live like Jews?"

Apostle Peter and even Barnabas were "*not in step with the truth of the gospel.*" Although some find it difficult, we need to recognize that the progress of revelation was ongoing even after the cross, even after Pentecost, and even after the apostolic council in Acts 15. Paul carried genuine apostolic authority which the other apostles came to respect. What was the issue? The primary issue is one of Paul's main themes and takes up considerable space in his epistles; the current state of the Mosaic Law. The same old questions: "What is a Jew? What is a Gentile? And then, what is a Christian?

While reading N.T. Wright on Christian history from 30-150AD I very interested by his observation. First, Christian sources of history during this time frame is considerably less than what we have for Judaism. We have no Christian Josephus. There is a serious lack of historical documents. Because I am committed to a long term view of God's kingdom on earth and also progressive understanding of our New Testament, I have little doubt that in future years archeologists will make discoveries which will assist in closing this historical gap. Maybe a person reading this will become an archaeologist and discover new historical documents. Yet, we can make certain conclusions about the Christians living in this time frame.

NT Wright:

These events form a chain stretching across a century in which, time after time, the Roman authorities found Christians (as they found the Jews) a social and political threat or nuisance, and took action against them. The Christians, meanwhile, do not seem to have taken refuge in the defense that they were merely a private club for the advancement of personal piety. They continued to proclaim their allegiance to a Christ who was a "king" in a sense which precluded allegiance to Caesar, even if his kingdom was not to be conceived on the model of Caesar's. This strange belief, so Jewish and yet so non-Jewish (since it lead the Christians to defend no city, adhere to no Mosaic code, circumcise no male children) was, as we shall see, a central characteristic of the whole movement, and as such a vital key to its character.[46]

According to Wright, what was a "central characteristic" of the early Christian movement? It can be summarized simply; they adhered to "NO MOSAIC CODE."

The history of our generation may be summarized as "Christians are confused about the covenants, some observe parts of the Mosaic code, others want both the civil and moral code obeyed and yet others are convinced the old covenant and all its laws have passed away." We certainly do not speak with one voice on these matters. My prayer is that soon, it can be said of the church, "They adhere only to the laws of Christ, written on hearts by the Holy Spirit."

Paul explains his position on the law:

Galatians 2:15-16

We ourselves are Jews by birth and not Gentile sinners; [16] yet we know that a person is not justified by works of the law but through faith in Jesus Christ, so we also have believed in Christ Jesus, in order to be justified by faith in Christ and not by works of the law, because by works of the law no one will be justified.

Paul's beginning argument is, even though they were Jews, they would not be justified by the works of the law. Only *"through faith*

---

[46] NT Wright, The New Testament and the People of God, Fortress Press, Minneapolis, Minnesota, 1992, p. 355

in Jesus Christ" can one be justified. This must be established, because for Paul, by the *"works of the law no one will be justified."*

Paul's next point is found in Chapter three. He points to receiving the Holy Spirit in defense of his *"truth of the gospel."*

> O foolish Galatians! Who has bewitched you? It was before your eyes that Jesus Christ was publicly portrayed as crucified. [2] Let me ask you only this: Did you receive the Spirit by works of the law or by hearing with faith? [3] Are you so foolish? Having begun by the Spirit, are you now being perfected by the flesh? [4] Did you suffer so many things in vain—if indeed it was in vain? [5] Does he who supplies the Spirit to you and works miracles among you do so by works of the law, or by hearing with faith? (Gal.3:1-5)

Paul is convinced the Galatians are *'bewitched.'* The word translated *'bewitched'* is the Greek word *"baskaino."* According to Strong's it means "to be fascinated" and according to Thayer it means "charmed." Maybe not as strong as many English translations imply, but Paul was rightly concerned about this because they had been fooled by a false view of the gospel.

He then asks a simple question. "How did you receive the Spirit?" Was the gift of the Spirit given because you kept the law? No! The Spirit is given in accordance with *"hearing with faith."* Receiving the Spirit is the reason for the *"miracles among you."* Paul builds his case for the sons of God being created through faith by bringing up Abraham. *"Knowing then that it is those of faith who are the sons of Abraham (3:7)."*

Those living under the Law of Moses were under a curse for disobedience. Are we as Christians under penalty for breaking the old covenant law? Paul makes it clear, *"Christ redeemed us from the curse of the law (3:13)."*

Galatians 3:23-25

Now before faith came, we were held captive under the law, imprisoned until the coming faith would be revealed. [24] So then, the law was our guardian until Christ came, in order that we might be justified by faith. [25] But now that faith has come, we are no longer under a guardian.

Paul builds his case by using words "captive" and "imprisoned." For Paul being under the law was like being a prisoner (and Paul knew about 1st century prisons).

The Law of Moses is likened to a guardian. A function of the guardian was taking the child to his teacher. Paul paints a picture he hopes the Galatians heed. The Law was our path, our means of seeing our teacher (God). Now since Christ we no longer need someone taking our hand and leading us to God. Through Christ we have free and unhindered access to our heavenly father.

When we keep Old Testament laws we are saying in essence, Christ is not enough, we still need guardians.

Paul then states a truth of the gospel which shook the known world. *"There is neither Jew nor Greek, there is neither slave nor free, there is no male and female, for you are all one in Christ Jesus (3:28).*

This offends everyone. The Greeks are offended (they are smarter than others). The Romans are offended (they had many slaves). All males were offended (for obvious reasons). And most of all, the Jews were offended. The removal of class distinctions was unthinkable and dangerous. This kind of thinking causes revolutions, overthrows governments, debunks religions, and causes overall havoc to society. Yet, this is the gospel! It was then and it is now.

With the removal of class distinctions it is beneficial we examine nationalism, our corporate divisions. The line between patriotism and nationalism is thin. We should be proud of our nation and work for its improvement. We enjoy our culture and way of life and will defend it when necessary; we need patriots. What we do not need is nationalism. When pride of our nation becomes arrogant and provides ammunition for prejudices then we are in sin and violate a basic tenant of our faith. Nationalism views other nations as inferior as racism view different races as fundamentally inferior. It is an exaggeration of one's own importance in comparison with others. It is the cause of most wars and an enemy of Christ's kingdom.

Paul speaks seriously to the Galatians and implores them not to follow the Law of Moses, because there are serious consciences for those who do.

Joe McIntyre makes an excellent comment on "flesh" and "Spirit."

"The law was for a people living in the flesh. The carnal mind and the body were in agreement and in rebellion and the law was to teach them what sin was. In Gal. 4:1-4 Paul distinguishes between "slaves" under Law, and "sons" who have the Spirit of the Son in them and are heirs of God and joint-heirs with Christ. Paul says in Romans we are no longer in the flesh but in the spirit if the Spirit of Christ dwells in us. It appears we are still capable, even in Christ and having the Spirit, of walking in the flesh, but we needn't."[47]

Hebrews 8:13

In speaking of a new covenant, he makes the first one obsolete. And what is becoming obsolete and growing old is ready to vanish away.

Hebrews 8:13 removes any doubt we are once and for all time free from the Mosaic Law. It leaves little room to reinstate them at a later time (Dispensationalism) or pick laws we prefer and make them binding upon Christians (Covenant Theology). What is missed all too often in the echoes of eschatology is an understanding regarding the time period of *"becoming obsolete"* and *"ready to vanish away."* The author of Hebrews recognizes the *"first"* covenant as

---

[47]   Joe McIntyre, From a personal email, 2014

"becoming obsolete." This seems odd given Jesus finished his redemptive work on the cross over thirty years prior. The heart of the old covenant and its authority was removed through the cross. What then was left of the first covenant? First, the theological battle over the Law of Moses was continuing. This battle was being won by Apostle Paul and others, yet, it was not complete. Second, and the most important, while the Second Temple was still standing, the shell of the old covenant was visible to all. Animals were being sacrificed and the old priesthood still functioned.

The temple represented the old covenant. Its presence was an ongoing statement. Just maybe, a new religion combining Jesus and the Law will win the day? No, says the author, it will *"vanish away."* As this was written only a few years before the Temple's destruction it is highly likely that the author was thinking of Jesus' prophecy in Matthew 24. Even though others were mocking and wondering if Jesus would keep his word (II Peter 3:4 *"Where is the promise of his coming?"*) and return in power and glory in his kingdom (Matthew 10:23, Matthew 16:28), he knew by the Spirit that the time of the complete demise of the Mosaic age and law was quickly arriving. When did it arrive? The age of Moses ended with the complete destruction of Jerusalem and the Temple. This happened when Jesus returned in Spirit to judge apostate Israel in 70AD. From that day forward no one confused the faith of Christians with Judaism. It was a time of clear separation. The old covenant served its purpose and is fulfilled.

If the moral law is binding for Christians and this includes the 10 commandments, then, what is our duty to the Sabbath?

"For many, the whole issue comes to the question of the Sabbath and whether it is an abiding demand. We would argue that Covenant Theology's shift of the Sabbath from Saturday to Sunday is exegetically unwarranted and that it further renders its "unchanged-ableness of the Decalogue" argument null and void. We would affirm rather that the Sabbath had a prophetic function in its anticipation of the gospel rest enjoyed by all who are in Christ, both now and in eternity (Heb.4)."[48]

Is the Sabbath part of Moral Law or should we change the Ten Commandments to nine and reclassify keeping the Sabbath to the Civil Law? Once we begin tinkering with the Mosaic Law and attempt to create separate divisions, it causes more problems than it solves.

As I studied the Mosaic Law and how Israel responded over the centuries, it is not difficult to conclude this was not God's intentions from the beginning. The Law came through Moses because they failed to be what he desired for them, which is becoming a "kingdom of priests" (Ex. 19:6).

Christians now are under a better covenant and the Spirit is within us. As we follow the Spirit the moral laws of God will be kept. God does not lead believers into sin. When people claim the "Spirit told me" and it violates the moral laws of God, then they are deceived. God's Holy Spirit can be trusted to lead us into a walk of holiness.

Exodus 19:6

[6]And you shall be to me a kingdom of priests and a holy nation. These are the words that you shall speak to the people of Israel.

What would a kingdom of priests look like? Certainly, much different than a people under the Mosaic code. Are we again seeing a collective Adam taking the low road?

The new covenant reveals what a kingdom of priests looks like. We have the access, we have the calling, we have the Spirit, and we were cleansed of sin and equipped for everything God desires for us. Again, are we settling for the low road, settling for what we think best? When the church across the nations receives a revelation of the new covenant, then, the world will see a kingdom of priests.

---

[48]   Fred G. Zaspel, A Brief Explanation of "New Covenant Theology," www.biblicalstudies

Chapter 9

Glorious Covenant
and Matthew 5:17-18

Do not think that I have come to abolish the Law or the
Prophets; I have not come to abolish them but to fulfill
them. For truly, I say to you, until heaven and earth pass
away, not an iota, not a dot, will pass from the Law until
all is accomplished (Matthew 5:17-18).

Even though we are continuing chapter eight, the words of Jesus as
recorded in Matthew five deserves additional attention. These words
have puzzled Bible interpreters over the centuries. Nevertheless,
they are key to an understanding of the relationship between the old
and new covenant. Did Jesus abolish the Law of Moses? No, says
Jesus, he came to *"fulfill"* not only the law but also the Prophets. If
Jesus did not destroy the law, then, are we still under the law? Paul
says we are not under law (Rom. 6:13). Who is right? How should
we understand the words of Jesus?

There are several contenders for rightly understanding the words of
Jesus in Matthew 5:17. We will briefly state the position of each and
not engage in pages of explanation (which this passage often
inspires).

1. Dispensationalism

Dispensationalism teaches that in the current dispensation (church
age) Christians are free from the Law.

*There are only three basic options in regard to the question of what
law must one follow as a Christian: (1) the saint must observe all of
the Mosaic Law as it fully applies today without any variations (no
Christian theology supports this position as it would require
sacrifices and a return to Judaism), (2) the saint must observe some*

of the Mosaic Law with some variations as given by the adjustments from the New Testament (most Covenantal theologians adopt this ideology), and (3) the saint must only observe the New Covenant law of Christ as given by Christ and explained by the apostles (Dispensational theologians, a modified Lutheran theology, and New Covenant theology supports this view).[49]

The saints must observe only new covenant law. Since this is the position of dispensationalism, I should have no issue. Yet, I do. Because they divide the history of salvation into many dispensations, the Mosaic Law is not finished; it only takes a break during the dispensation of the church age. At this point dispensationalism and its position concerning Mosaic Law and the millennial kingdom are confusing. There seems to be no universal agreement, yet certain things are clear; in the Millennium animal sacrifices are reinstituted as a memorial.

*The building of the temple will be the most important construction project in the Millennial Age for all Jews… In Ezekiel, we read that the Jews in the Millennial Kingdom will be required to **keep the Law of Moses** including making animal sacrifices (Ezekiel 45, 46). Most Christians find it very difficult to understand why God would reintroduce animal sacrifices under the New Covenant. Once we appreciate that the **New Covenant does not abolish** the Law of God given to Moses, then it is not difficult to understand why Millennial Jews will keep these sacrificial laws.*"[50]

So in one place the new covenant believers are to obey the "law of Christ" and in another place dispensationalists says the opposite. The previous author continues with his dispensational explanation:

*The main point to understand about animal sacrifices, whether in the Old Testament or in the Millennial Kingdom, is that their purpose is as **a reminder of sins**… Animal sacrifices will be **a powerful reminder** to the nation of Israel and a witness to all of the*

[49] Keith Sherlin, Essential Christianity Ministries, http://www.essentialchristianity.com
[50] David and Zoë Sulem, God's Plan for All, http://www.godsplanforall.com

*Gentile nations that the only begotten Son of God, Jesus Christ, died on the cross to forgive the sins of the whole world, and that Jesus Christ's blood alone takes away sins... In the Millennial Kingdom, God will make a New Covenant with the nation of Israel... God will grant to every Jew, the gift of God given faith to believe in Jesus... It is important to understand that the New Covenant, though it replaces the Old Covenant, **does not abolish** the Law of God given to Moses. Under the New Covenant, the Israelites will be able to **keep the Law of Moses** in the **newness of the Spirit** because of the gift of God's Righteousness.*

*God has kept the Israelites a distinct and separate nation from the Gentile nations, both racially through the descendants of the line of Jacob, and religiously through the Mosaic Law. **The Law of Moses is always important** to a Jew, whether he is an unconverted Jew **or a born again**, converted Jew. All of the many Jews who believed in Jesus Christ during the early Christian era remained zealous for the Law of Moses after their conversion (Acts 21:20). The Law of Moses was very important to Apostle Paul and he kept it. He says that the law is holy, just and good (Romans 7:12).*[51]

The reason dispensationalists can have their cake and eat it too stems from their separation of Israel from the church. The church is not under the law because we are not under the new covenant spoken of by Jeremiah. So, when they say the new covenant does not abolish the Law of Moses, they are speaking of Israel in their 1,000 year Millennium.

To fully engage with a rebuttal is beyond my purpose here. It would literally take a book to correct the multitude of faulty theology and exegesis just in this short quote. My purpose is to show even though dispensationalists propose discontinuity to the Law of Moses, as its basic premise, in reality, it accepts continuity. Even though our discussion wandered from our text in Matthew, it was necessary to

[51]   Ibid.

see the overall understanding of dispensationalism and how it handles the Law of Moses.

2. Covenant Theology

Reformed theologian John Gill writing in his <u>John Gill's Exposition of the Bible</u> concerning the words of Jesus in Matthew says, *"By "the law' is meant the moral law."*[52] I find this rush to judgment a little simplistic for my taste. What in the text says Jesus is referring to ONLY the "moral law?" John Gill is committed to Covenant Theology and sees the Mosaic Laws in three parts (civil, ceremonial, and moral). But Jesus did not say only the "Law" but added "The Prophets." I believe Jesus was viewing the whole of Old Testament Scripture, not just one small aspect of the Law of Moses.

Reformed author R.C. Sproul gives us insight how covenant theology divides the law and the gospel.

Reformed thinkers, however, traditionally view God's law more positively. Yes, the Reformed tradition has said that we must sharply distinguish law and gospel—but only in regards to our justification.[53]

If you follow Covenant Theology, the Mosaic Law is not for salvation, but it is useful for sanctification. Yes, we are saved by grace through faith, but once saved, our maturity and growth as a Christian depends on keeping the law. The majority holding Covenant Theology interpret the law as the moral law; whereas Reformed Theonomists would argue for considerably more.

3. New Covenant Theology:

"Contextual indicators in Matthew 5 run along these same lines. First, as pointed out previously, "fulfill" stands in contrast (alla) to "destroy," which has the sense of invalidating or destroying that for

---

[52]   John Gill, John Gill's Exposition of the Bible, http://www.biblestudytools.com

[53]   R.C. Sproul, Ligonier Ministries, Law and Gospel, http://www.ligonier.org

which something was intended. The law will not fall to the ground."[54]

New Covenant Theology adherents find the key in the word "fulfill." Jesus fulfilled the purpose for which he came. The Law and the Prophets are not wiped clean as to be forgotten, but are the very thing Jesus came to fulfill. Jesus does not come in a vacuum, he comes as Israel's Messiah and is directly connected to the Old Testament. Therefore, to continue keeping the Law of Moses and think the "Prophets" are speaking of yet another day, would be a great mistake. Jesus is the one to; "fulfill' both the law and the prophets.

New Covenant Theology makes a good case. I agree *"fulfill"* does not mean we are to continue keeping the Mosaic Law but leads us to Jesus' words *"until all is accomplished."*

3. Better Covenant Theology

Even though it is too early in its development to make any final conclusions for Better Covenant Theology, I will make several observations which hopefully will help in understanding Matthew 5.

Four Questions

I will summarize by asking four questions.

Question 1
Is the Law of Moses continuing or it is abrogated?

The lengthy doctrinal debates center mostly on this question. My conclusion is close to the position of New Covenant Theology. To continue to keep the Mosaic Law would be saying in essence, "We are still waiting for the Messiah." The Law is not abolished, it is there as an eternal testimony to the one who came to fulfill it.

---

[54] Fred G. Zaspel, New Covenant Theology and the Mosaic Law, http://www. biblestudies.com

Keeping the letter of the law (II cor. 3) serves no purpose and according to Paul is a dangerous substitute for grace (Gal. 5:1-6).

Under grace we do not murder, steal or bear false witness. Nevertheless, our life is not shaped by following the rules of Moses but by being led by the Spirit who leads us into holiness and truth.

Question 2
Why did Jesus come to earth?

The second question I have and often ignored (although the New Covenant Theology position comes close) is, "What is the connection between the words "*I came*" to the reminder of the sentence." I believe the key point made by Jesus centers around the purposes for his coming. He did not come to throw away the entirety of the Scripture. He did not want them abolished because they pointed to him. He is what the Old Testament saints looked forwards to (Israel's Messiah and Kingdom). It is necessary to see the Law and the Prophets as the body of Scripture pointing to Israel's Messiah. If we erased the Old Testament, Jesus would have no context for his coming. The fulfillment is in the person of Jesus to which the law pointed. He is the fulfillment of everything Moses and the Prophets spoke of. How could he abolish the written word of God? He did not come to "abolish" but to "fulfill." It is necessary to see the Law and the Prophets as the body of Scripture pointing to Israel's Messiah.

In my opinion this statement is eschatological. Jesus' purpose in coming cannot be separated from the arrival of his kingdom. The kingdom Yahweh told Israel was coming, is now here. Jesus' first words were the "kingdom of God is at hand" (Matt. 4:17).

Since Jesus came to establish God's reign, any discussion of keeping the Law must include the nature of the kingdom. Jesus as the enthroned King is ruling over creation. What is the nature of this kingdom? Does it continue enforcing the Mosaic Law? Or is there another law which sets kingdom people free from the burden of Moses and his long list of rules (remember 613 of them)?

My view is yes, Jesus sets us free, not just free from 50% or 90% of the Mosaic Law, but 100%. If we are bound to just 1% then we are bound to keep it all. There is no justification for the division of the Law into three parts so we can pick and choose. **The Mosaic Law— all of it—was nailed to the cross with Christ.**

Paul stated it best in Galatians. *"For freedom Christ has set you free; stand firm therefore, and do submit again to a yoke of slavery."* For the new covenant believer submitting to the Mosaic Law is akin to slavery. This points us in the right direction, Jesus came to fulfill all Scripture and to set us free to live in his kingdom.

Question 3
How long must we keep the Law of Moses?

Without a preterist interpretation the answer is almost embarrassing. Jesus makes it clear: *"For truly, I say to you, until heaven and earth pass away, not an iota, not a dot, will pass from the Law until all is accomplished."*

Jesus shuts the door on the picking out the greater moral laws for continuation. Even the smallest law is to continue *"UNTIL all is accomplished."* This puts the exegete in a corner. If we interpret "heaven and earth" as literal then the whole of the Mosaic Law continues today because the literal heaven and earth remain. Yet, if we view heaven and earth through the lens of the New Testament a more plausible exegesis is available.

Heaven and earth cannot be seen as literal in this passage. Since no theological system teaches Christians are under the entirety of Mosaic Law, then, how can we understand this? There is only one reasonable alternative; heaven and earth is used as a symbol and has passed away. But what does it symbolize?

God in the creation made the "heavens and the earth." This is the first creation. In the book of Isaiah he predicts a new heavens and a new earth (Is. 65:17-25). Reading what the Prophet said narrows our choices for a time frame. It cannot be heaven or in the post-resurrection period, because people still die; even though human life is extended. The conditions Isaiah saw, I believe, is the continual growth of the kingdom of God. It began as a mustard seed in the first century and grows until all nations become followers of Jesus. So according to Isaiah, since the coming of the Messiah we are living in the new creation, the new heavens and new earth.

The old creation represented the old covenant and the new creation represents the new covenant. When the New Testament authors write about the passing of the old heavens and earth it is their way of saying the old covenant is passing away. II Peter 3 is another place which speaks of this passing way of the heavens and earth. In my book Glorious Kingdom there is a chapter devoted to this passage. My conclusion then, and now, is that the heavens and earth which Peter wrote about and what Jesus spoke of in Matthew 5, are not the physical earth or heavens but is symbolic of the passing of the old covenant and establishing the new creation; the new covenant.

Jonathan Welton:

This illuminates Jesus' statement in Matthew 5 that "until heaven and earth disappear, not the smallest letter, not the least stroke of a pen, will by any means disappear from the Law until everything is accomplished" (Matt. 5:18). It is obvious that Jesus could not have been referring to the literal end of the world, because after AD 70 it was literally impossible to keep every aspect of the Law, since the priesthood and temple no longer existed. Therefore the Law disappeared when "heaven and earth," which is to say, the Temple System, disappeared. Knowing the history of this phrase helps us understand what Jesus was actually referring to. Jesus picked up the same concept later in Matthew 24, where He prophesied the destruction of the temple. Near the end of the discussion, and he said, "Heaven and earth will pass away, but my words will never pass away" (Matt. 24:35). In other words, the temple and the old covenant system inextricably linked to it would pass away, but His words and the new covenant would endure forever. The people listening to Him in that day would have understood exactly what He meant when He said that.[55]

Welton makes an excellent point. How can anyone keep the Law of Moses after the temple was torn down? Jesus was clear: until *"heaven and earth pass away"* we must keep the Law of Moses intact.

The law passed away, it is dead, and therefore, even though it is useful for learning more about Jesus and the kingdom, it no longer remains as an authoritative word for new covenant Christians.

Heaven and earth is a symbol of covenant. The old covenant was the first creation. The new covenant is the new heaven and earth. Some object that a world filled with evil cannot be the new earth. But our logic does not interpret Scripture. Paul calls those in Christ as a new creation (II Cor. 5:17). We are the first fruits of this new earth. Are we perfect yet? Neither is the physical earth.

The words "new creation" remind us that the old creation has passed away. God has begun renewing his new world. It is far from completion. God is not finished with his original goal to renew the world through his people. The first agenda was to renew his people (through the ministry of Christ) and now we are responsible to work and see the earth renewed. **The new covenant is eschatology in action!**

Christians for several decades have been on the wrong side of most environmental issues. We are stewards of the earth and it has a long future; therefore, Christians should be on the front lines to make sure we are not polluting our rivers, contaminating the soil, and choking ourselves with smog. Yes, we need good science, but good theology on the kingdom should lead us, not the agendas of political parties.

---

[55] Jonathan Welton, Understanding the Whole Bible, 2014, p. 276

What about heaven? What was wrong with the old heaven? We have a new heaven because of the ascension; we now have a man (the man Christ Jesus) in heaven.

Question 4
Is Moses Useful?

The simple answer is yes. With everything said about the Mosaic Law we must not conclude that Moses and his Law are no longer useful. We will be studying the Mosaic Law for centuries in order to see Christ. Jesus said the Law spoke of him and we are only beginning to see all the types, shadows and references which shine a greater light on him and his kingdom.

Chapter 10

The Glorious Covenant
Abraham & David

Abraham

Does the new covenant fulfill the promises to Abraham? Is old Israel still waiting for the complete promise? Many Christians think so and are giving large sums of money to relocate Jews back to Israel. Are we witnessing prophecy being fulfilled? Should we give money to send Jews back to their homeland? I would find better places to sow into the kingdom. And if dispensationalism is correct (God forbid) then Christians are sending thousands of Jews back to Israel only to be slaughtered in the Great Tribulation.

New Testament Scriptures about Abraham are extensively covered in my book Glorious Kingdom; here we will focus on the city he was looking for. First, the Old Testament tells us when the promise of the land was fulfilled.

Joshua 23:14-16

"And now I am about to go the way of all the earth, and you know in your hearts and souls, all of you, that not one word has failed of all the good things that the LORD your God promised concerning you. All have come to pass for you; not one of them has failed. [15] But just as all the good things that the LORD your God promised concerning you have been fulfilled for you, so the LORD will bring upon you all the evil things, until he has destroyed you from off this good land that the LORD your God has given you, [16] if you transgress the covenant of the LORD your God, which he commanded you, and go and serve other gods and bow down to them. Then the anger of the LORD will be kindled against you, and you shall perish quickly from off the good land that he has given to you."

How many promises were waiting for fulfillment at the end of Joshua's time? Not one, *"All have come to pass."* This may be one of the most forgotten passages in the Bible. The promise of the *"land"* is fulfilled. The big question is, "How long will you stay in the land?" If Israel transgress' the covenant then *"You shall perish quickly from off the good land."*

Once we get to the New Testament the whole 'Israel returning to the land' issue takes a new direction. There is not a single verse in the New Testament where Israel is said to return to the land and fulfill the promises to Abraham.

So what was Abraham looking for? If not a physical land, then what?

Hebrews 11:8-12

By faith Abraham obeyed when he was called to go out to a place that he was to receive as an inheritance. And he went out, not knowing where he was going. ^{9} By faith he went to live in the land of promise, as in a foreign land, living in tents with Isaac and Jacob, heirs with him of the same promise. ^{10} For he was looking forward to the city that has foundations, whose designer and builder is God. ^{11} By faith Sarah herself received power to conceive, even when she was past the age, since she considered him faithful who had promised. ^{12} Therefore from one man, and him as good as dead, were born descendants as many as the stars of heaven and as many as the innumerable grains of sand by the seashore.

Abraham was not exclusively seeking a small section of real estate in the Middle East. Once we establish this, the New Testament can lead us. What city was he looking for? Scripture says he was looking for a city with *"foundations."*

Our first response is "Abraham is looking for heaven." Yet, let's look a little deeper.

Where else can we find Scripture that talks about foundations?

Isaiah 28:16

Therefore thus says the Lord GOD, "Behold, I am the one who has laid as a foundation in Zion, a stone, a tested stone, a precious cornerstone, of a sure foundation.

Seven hundred years before Jesus we have a prophecy about the intentions of the Father. He intends to build the true house of God and therefore he must have a foundation stone, a precious and tested stone, and a true cornerstone. **The city which arises from this foundation is Zion.**

Jesus, Israel's Messiah is the tested stone. He was tested and was found faithful. He was the cornerstone to build a great house.

Psalms 118:22-23

The stone that the builders rejected has become the cornerstone. This is the LORD's doing; it is marvelous in our eyes.

Going back several hundred years before Isaiah we again read about a stone which becomes the cornerstone. In Acts chapter four Peter makes clear that everyone knows who the "builders" are and exactly who is the "cornerstone."

Acts 4:10-11

Let it be known to all of you and to all the people of Israel that by the name of Jesus Christ of Nazareth, whom you crucified, whom God raised from the dead—by him this man is standing before you well. This Jesus is the stone that was rejected by you, the builders, which has become the cornerstone.

Jesus is the cornerstone and the believing people of Israel (eschatological Israel) are the builders.

When Peter writes his epistle he makes this point again.

I Peter 2:4-7

As you come to him, a living stone rejected by men but in the sight of God chosen and precious, [5] you yourselves like living stones are being built up as a spiritual house, to be a holy priesthood, to offer spiritual sacrifices acceptable to God through Jesus Christ. [6] For it stands in Scripture: "Behold, I am laying in Zion a stone, a cornerstone chosen and precious, and whoever believes in him will not be put to shame." So the honor is for you who believe, but for those who do not believe, "The stone that the builders rejected has become the cornerstone."

The picture is becoming clear. God is building a new house. Jesus is the foundation for this new household. The old covenant produced a temple of stone but the new is a temple of 'living stones.' There is no turning back, there is no need and NO desire to build once again a temple of stone.

Paul explains how this new house built upon the "cornerstone" is a "dwelling of God in the Spirit."

Ephesians 2:19-22

So then you are no longer strangers and aliens, but you are fellow citizens with the saints and members of the household of God, [20] built on the foundation of the apostles and prophets, Christ Jesus himself being the cornerstone, [21] in whom the whole structure, being joined together, grows into a holy temple in the Lord. [22] In him you also are being built together into a dwelling place for God by the Spirit.

Paul adds new information; he says the foundation includes "apostles and prophets." Jesus is the main foundation as he is the cornerstone yet this new household is also built upon ministries of the Church.

So what was Abraham seeking? Was he seeing heaven or was he seeking a glorious church-the city of Zion; built upon the foundation, the cornerstone; the coming Messiah? My conclusion; **Abraham was looking for the Church; the city of Zion; the New Jerusalem.**

This revelation is crucial for new covenant theology. We are walking in Abraham's vision. We are fulfilling the covenant and promises made to him.

David

II Samuel 7:16

"And your house and your kingdom shall be made sure forever before me. Your throne shall be established forever."

"We can be assured as followers of Jesus that every word given to David will happen in and through the church."[56] The covenant given to David is fulfilled by Jesus, where he sits on David's throne in heaven ruling over his creation. We will not arrive at a glorious covenant if we push to the future the Davidic covenant. This makes dispensationalists a little crazy. In a rebuttal of Acts 2 as a proof text for the current reign of Jesus, Ryrie says:

"Actually, what Peter is arguing for is the identification of Jesus of Nazareth as the Davidic king, since Jesus, not David, was raised from the dead and exalted to the right hand of the Father. He does not add that He is reigning as the Davidic king. That will happen in the future millennial kingdom. If it is so clear that our Lord is reigning now as the Davidic king in the inaugural fulfillment of the

---

[56]   Stan Newton, Glorious Kingdom, Vision Publishing, Ramona, CA., 2012, p. 54

Davidic covenant, why is that only alluded to in Acts 2? Links and similarities between reigns do not make clear an equality between the Davidic reign and Christ's present rule. "[57]

Ryrie's statement leaves me bewildered. It shows to what extent dispensationalists go to twist Scripture to their match their theology. Yes, we all have 'troubling verses' but to take a simple statement of Scripture and push its fulfillment far in the future, is just plain wrong and bad exegesis. The whole point of Peter's message that had just happened (Pentecost) is the fulfillment of Joel and the prophets. Jesus was raised from the dead; therefore; the Spirit has arrived! The kingdom has arrived!

The subject of David and its relative theology is the material of many books. What needs to be pointed out, I believe, is the connection to his promised kingdom and the new covenant. I see this in the story of David pitching his own tent to showcase the Ark of the Covenant.

Ark of the Covenant

The events of David's life are the stuff of great fiction. A great chapter would be his adventures of bringing home the Ark of the Covenant. Everyone knows the Ark belongs in the tent fashioned after the instructions of Moses. The Ark belonged in the section behind the curtain, unseen except for a few priests. Something happened one day which only could be accomplished by a king. He passed by the road to Gibeon and headed to a new location; Mt. Zion. There, he pitched a tent and placed the Ark of the Covenant. What happened? A revival of worship; free, spontaneous, and open to all.

As far as we can tell, and the Scripture is not clear, it seems like there was no curtain separating the Ark of the Covenant from the eyes of the people. Upon entering the tent everyone would witness and experience the very presence of Yahweh. There was no

---

[57] Charles C. Ryrie, Dispensationalism, Moody Press, Chicago, Illinois, 1995, p. 168

membership, no limitations who could enter. It was one of the most amazing times in all of Old Testament history.

I believe David by the power of the Spirit jumped ahead one thousand years and experienced new covenant worship. He totally ignored the rules of old covenant. Only a king could achieve such a massive change. The breaking of numerous Mosaic Laws never bothered David as he experienced what most Old Testament people never achieved; the presence of God celebrated with freedom and joy.

Once the Temple of Solomon was finished, God came in the normal manner and everything reverted back to keeping the laws of Moses. David lived in a small window where he and others entered a realm of spirit where new covenant laws for worship were in effect. This is a clear portrayal in the Old Testament showing how Christ's kingdom functions under a new covenant. The kingdom of God in its newest form looks significantly different from its old covenant expression.

Chapter 11

The Glorious Covenant is Grace

If the chapters were arranged in their importance this one deserves to be near the top. We cannot speak the words "new covenant" without thinking of grace. Grace is the spiritual energy behind the new covenant. Grace reveals the heart of God. Grace reveals the love of Jesus. And grace should be the authentic nature of the church. The old covenant was law. The new covenant is grace.

Baker's Evangelical Dictionary of Biblical Theology provided us the legal understanding of Grace.

Perhaps the most dominant metaphor with which grace is associated is the legal metaphor of justification. We see the two linked in two very important passages in which grace is used in Paul. Romans 3:23-24 states quite clearly that all have fallen short of the glory of God and are "justified freely by his grace through the redemption that came by Christ Jesus..." Hence the unmerited favor of God buys us legal freedom from our sin and cancels the sentence of guilt the judge has had to declare in order "to be just and the one who justified those who have faith in Jesus" (v. 26). [58]

The subject of grace and our justification is covered as much as any subject in the New Testament. Recent New Testament scholars such as NT Wright are questioning traditional views; Wright's mammoth 2200 page new book, Paul and the Faithfulness of God, presents an outstanding academic debate.

Yet, for our limited scope we want to recognize God's revelation is always progressive. We can expect future books on grace because

---

[58] Baker's Evangelical Dictionary of Biblical Theology, Edited by Walter A. Elwell, Baker Press, Grand Rapids, Michigan, 1996

all revelation is progressive. Grace lays at the foundation of the new covenant. We are saved by grace and we walk by grace.

Even though grace is given to every believer, history shows that Christians often find it difficult to show similar grace to others. We seem to be harder on ourselves (those in the church) than God is on us.

Yet, for our purposes here, we must narrow our discussion. Since grace is the Spirit of the new covenant, it separates us from the legal system of the previous covenant. To write a book on covenant and not write about God's grace through faith would add speculation that a new theology is being offered which ignores the cross. Let me state it clearly; grace is the story of salvation, it is the central element of the new covenant. This is assumed in everything I write. It is not necessary for it to be restated. Yet, a few statements about how 'grace' is back in the news again is warranted.

Grace is having a revival these days; not only a fresh theology on grace but the experience of grace. Seems strange, but with the church majoring in minors for centuries, it is overdue. I have little doubt the pendulum will swing too far, but we need not worry, these things correct themselves. If we join those attempting to stop this "grace movement" we may kill the very thing the church needs. Currently there is great debate on the subject of grace. Books are being released warning the church of the errors of "hyper grace." Then, other books are written defending true "biblical grace." Once the theological debate settles down, in my opinion, the church will possess a greater knowledge and experience of grace.

Missing in much of this debate is how grace, the new covenant, and the establishing of Christ's kingdom flow together. The Bible tells us to come to the *"throne of Grace"* (Heb. 4:16). Thrones are seats of authority; grace has authority, it has the power to change people. Not by forcing people to obey laws, but by its very nature it brings people into relationship with God and love for those who also love God. Normally we tend to equate authority with strength and maybe even harshness, but the administration of Messiah's kingdom flows through grace. If we desire to move in authority we move first in grace.

When grace is stressed as arriving with Jesus there are those (Covenant Theology) who feel that to overly stress grace under the new covenant, steals grace from the old covenant. No one is saying God withheld grace under the old covenant. God's grace is seen everyone, with Noah, with Moses, with the people of God wandering in the desert. Yet, when Jesus came in the flesh there was a new revelation of grace. There is now a higher level of grace. *"For the law was given through Moses; grace and truth came through Jesus Christ* (John 1:17)."

Ephesians 2:5-9

By grace you have been saved, [6] and raised us up with him and seated us with him in the heavenly places in Christ Jesus, [7] so that in the coming ages he might show the immeasurable riches of his grace in kindness toward us in Christ Jesus. [8] For by grace you have been saved through faith. And this is not your own doing; it is the gift of God, [9] not a result of works, so that no one may boast.

God in his unlimited grace not only saved us from our sins but raised us and has seated us with Christ in his place of enthronement. Grace releases God's love and purpose in the present and will in the coming ages show the *"immeasurable riches of his grace in kindness towards us."* Why are we seated in heavenly places? So we have a kingdom perspective now and the ages to come.

I Peter 4:10

As each has received a gift, use it to serve one another, as good stewards of God's varied grace.

As we serve each other let grace be our motivation. When we set out to fix fellow believers who in our eyes are not living or acting in an acceptable fashion, we come across as being superior. When people fail and are hurting, it is better to show them love and not place them under a greater burden of guilt. Even though God established authority in the church for discipline, it must be done according to Scripture. When people are hurting—often resulting from sin or failure—a flow of grace is the best way to restore them. The discipline from the Lord is often enough to bring about the required repentance, and when that occurs, people of grace need to be there to welcome them.

True new covenant living begins with a continued knowledge of God's grace toward us and extending it to others. When we forget the grace poured out on us we tend to place people under condemnation for not obeying certain laws. We love to create church laws, laws from tradition, and many are good to practice but they do not replace grace.

Grace is a gift. Jesus purchased grace for us though his cross. When we repent of our sins and embrace Jesus as God's son whom he raised from the dead, grace is poured into our lives. Christians are a testimony of grace.

Grace is beyond our expectations of justice. Grace is messy. Is it fair for a violent person who murders to experience salvation ten minutes before execution? Should anyone abusing children EVER be forgiven? What justice can there be when a swindler steals the life savings of an elderly couple? Where is the penalty for these horrendous crimes? Death does not seem enough. Yet, this is the story of grace.

Ephesians 1:7-10

In him we have redemption through his blood, the forgiveness of our trespasses, according to the riches of his grace, [8] which he lavished upon us, in all wisdom and insight [9] making known to us the mystery of his will, according to his purpose, which he set forth in Christ [10] as a plan for the fullness of time, to unite all things in him, things in heaven and things on earth.

As the final words in this short chapter, these same verses from <u>The Message</u> says it best.

> Because of the sacrifice of the Messiah, his blood poured out on the altar of the Cross, we're a free people—free of penalties and punishments chalked up by all our misdeeds. And not just barely free, either. *Abundantly* free! He thought of everything, provided for everything we could possibly need, letting us in on the plans he took such delight in making. He set it all out before us in Christ, a long-range plan in which everything would be brought together and summed up in him, everything in deepest heaven, everything on planet earth (The Message).

Chapter 12

The Glorious Covenant
is the Law of Christ

We arrive in our journey where Moses meets Christ. At least Moses' law meets Christ's law. This may be the most important chapter. Not because the Law of Christ is more important than grace, or understanding the "one people of God" or believing the "Mosaic Covenant is ended," or other subjects already covered. Its potential importance is because the subject of the Law of Christ is less known. Therefore, there is huge potential for growth in the church. I am not sure why we hear so little about the Law of Christ. We preach around the topic, we preach its essence; we just fail in connecting our thoughts to its name, "The Law of Christ."

Studying God's Law is not easy and it is vital to keep our goal in mind. Wells and Zaspel state it well.

"The study of divine law takes the student from many passages bristling with exegetical challenges to hermeneutical issues such as redemptive history and typology and on through to theological categories such as ecclesiology, soteriology, even eschatology. Most rewarding of all, as we should expect, the study finds its culmination in the person and work of Christ. It is to this end that our study should always lead us."[59]

I agree; studying God's Law must lead us to Christ. Divine law is often considered a single identity. When we think of God's Law, we automatically bring up Moses. Yet, the most important divine law is rarely mentioned; the Law of Christ. Why is that? The work of Christ, his miraculous birth, his amazing teaching, his death on the cross, his resurrection from the dead, and add his ascension and

---

[59]   Tom Wells, Fred Zaspel, New Covenant theology, New Covenant Media, Frederick, Maryland, 2002, p. 139

enthronement; there is not much room for another area of study in Christology. Yet, this missing element is why such confusion exists in the church. We love the salvation of Christ, but once saved, we have a variety of mixed-up ways of becoming a true disciple. Where is our book of rules? Local churches write their own. Denominations write laws. Tradition hands down many laws. And then, the greatest list of Laws is from Moses. Many Christians create their own book of rules from these various sources to have an objective standard to follow. But we forget the most important and the only one which really matters; the Law of Christ.

The Prophets and the Law of Christ?

Before we journey into the New Testament we will read what Isaiah wrote seven hundred years before Christ.

> Behold my servant, whom I uphold,
> my chosen, in whom my soul delights;
> **I have put my Spirit upon him**;
>   he will bring **forth justice to the nations**.
> ² He will not cry aloud or lift up his voice,
>   or make it heard in the street;
> ³ a bruised reed he will not break,
>   and a faintly burning wick he will not quench;
>   he will faithfully bring forth justice.
> ⁴ He will not grow faint or be discouraged
>   till he has established justice in the earth;
>   and **the coastlands wait for his law** (Isaiah 42:1-4).

Without question this is Messianic. Isaiah is describing the ministry of Jesus. He will have the Spirit upon him; he will bring forth justice to the nations and not grow faint or be discouraged until he has established justice in the earth. We have this promise from God. The last few words are thought-provoking and often overlooked. It says of the Messiah "the coastlands wait for his law."

What Law will the Messiah teach?

Before answering consider what Prophet Micah has to say.

> It shall come to pass in the **latter days**
> that the mountain of the house of the LORD
> shall be established as the highest of the mountains,
> and it shall be lifted up above the hills;
> and peoples shall flow to it,
> and many nations shall come, and say:
> "Come, let us go up to the mountain of the LORD,
> to the house of the God of Jacob,
> that he may teach us his ways
> and that we may walk in his paths ."
> **For out of Zion shall go forth the law**,
> and the word of the LORD from Jerusalem (Micah 4:1-2).

First, the events here begin in the "last days" which is when Jesus came to earth and the church was born. The "last days" according to Scripture is the final generation of the old covenant. It has nothing to say about any end of the world scenario.

Those familiar with the book of Hebrews should understand that the apostles saw Zion not in an Old Testament sense but from the new covenant perspective.

Hebrews 12:22

> But you have come to Mount Zion and to the city of the living God, the heavenly Jerusalem, and to innumerable angels in festal gathering.

Zion is where the new covenant church lives. We are Zion, the city of God; the New Jerusalem. What did Micah say? *"Out of Zion shall go forth the law."* What Law? The Law of Moses or the Law of Christ?

Any Jew reading Isaiah or Micah in the days of Jesus would know for a fact their Messiah would teach the only Law from God; the

Mosaic Law. This was one of the contentious points with Jesus; his handling of the Law.

If we are to see Jesus in the Law and the Prophets (as he told us) we must interpret this type of passage with New Testament understanding. If Malachi was the last word from God, then our answer is easy; but it was not.

Therefore, the people of God born into Messiah's body will be agents of "teaching the law." **What Law should we teach the nations? I am convinced that we are not to be teaching this Mosaic Law, but the Law of Christ.**

Hebrews 7:11

> Now if perfection had been attainable through the Levitical priesthood (for under it the people received the law), what further need would there have been for another priest to arise after the order of Melchizedek, rather than one named after the order of Aaron?

If we shorten the sentence and add a little interpretation it could read like this, "Now if perfection had been attainable 'under the law' what need would we have for **'another law.'**

Now we read verse 12: *"For when there is a change in the priesthood, there is necessarily **a change in the law as well**."* I have heard thousands of sermons over the years and listened to lectures from biblical scholars, and yet, I have never heard one mention of the possibility we are under a "new law" with the coming of the new covenant. Yet, I am convinced we have one, it is called the Law of Christ. Other astute interpreters will point to the Mosaic Law as not being replaced, as it means the "law" of the priesthood. Even if this is correct, there is still a change of both priesthood and law. Jesus is not a new type of priest and who then reverts back to the Mosaic Law. My position remains; when the new priest came (Jesus) he taught a new law.

When we look back at Jeremiah's prophecy, it says the laws will be written in our hearts instead of on stone. **Does that mean at salvation the new believer has all 613 Mosaic Laws written in their hearts?**

I do not know a single case of anyone being "born again" and having a great desire to obey the Mosaic code of laws. I have never heard of any testimony claiming after being born again they must:

"Go acquire a Canaanite slave and keep them."

"Kill an Amalek."

"Rush home and built a fence on their roof."

"Never lend money to a poor person."

"To tie the Bible to their head."

"To salt their sacrifice."

"At every new moon to offer a sacrifice."

"Stay close to home on Saturday."

You get the picture. The Holy Spirit under the new covenant is not actively writing the Mosaic code in our hearts!

Advocates of Covenant Theology would say, "No, not all the laws, just the Moral Laws are written on our hearts." Yet, is not keeping the Sabbath a moral law? How can we know what is "moral" as differentiated from the hundreds of civil and ceremonial laws?

The Laws written on our hearts is NOT the Mosaic Law but the Law of Christ.

I know this interpretation is a stretch for many. Yet, I believe it is how we must see the role of Holy Spirit in writing the "Law" on our hearts. Also, as a system of covenant, it distinguishes itself from all previous positions.

We know occasions where the Apostles interpreted what seemed like a clear prophecy from the Old Testament and changed the meaning entirely (Acts 15 is an example from Amos 9). Did Amos know his prophecy was about Gentiles coming into God's family? But that is how James and the apostles saw it.

This leads to a grand conclusion:

Hebrews 7:22

"This makes Jesus the guarantor of a better covenant."

We finally understand; our Walk in the Spirit in the new covenant is better than any covenant before. There is no need to mix the covenants, no need to keep anything of the old alive, or anything of this sort; in Jesus we have a **Better Covenant**.

Defining the Law of Christ

We have yet to define the "Law of Christ." Where is our list of rules? What does Apostle Paul mean by using this term? He certainly knew his readers would compare this new set of Laws with the Mosaic Law. Yet, we have no official list of Laws for new covenant living. To create a list we must carefully read and number each commandment. As previously said, the consensus of most scholars is there are 613 laws under the old covenant. How many Laws or commandments do we have in the New Testament? There is no similar consensus but here are some opinions.

"There are 1,050 commands in the New Testament for Christians to obey. Due to repetitions we can classify them under 69 headings. They cover every phase of man's life in his relationship to God and his fellowmen, now and hereafter. If obeyed, they will bring rich rewards here and forever; if disobeyed, they will bring condemnation and eternal punishment."[60]

---

[60] Christian Assemblies International, 1050 New Testament Commands, http://www.cai.org

If this list is accurate we just added 437 more laws than they had under the old covenant. We better get bigger refrigerators so we remind ourselves daily of our serious responsibility under the new covenant. According to this quote, we risk "eternal punishment" if we disobey. Ouch!

Another group who specializes in biblical research list 684 passages of Scripture containing commandments in the New Testament. We can assume, some verses contain more than one commandment.[61]

I will not include the list of 1050 commandments or the 684 passages (even though I included the 613 Mosaic Laws, because the majority of them are unknown to many Christians). My biggest question is, "Is this the core essence of being a Christian, following over 1,000 Laws—and walking in fear of "eternal punishment?" No, it is not!

The actual wording "Law of Christ" is used sparingly in the New Testament. Should we then, dismiss it as a major factor in determining how we view the new covenant? No! There are many topics in the Scriptures where there is no single phrase which brings together the complete teaching of the subject. Also, with the Law of Christ, even though the term is absent in many biblical discussions, the subject matter is the same.

The first use of the 'Law of Christ' is found in I Corinthians.

I Corinthians 9:19-21

For though I am free from all, I have made myself a servant to all, that I might win more of them. [20] To the Jews I became as a Jew, in order to win Jews. To those under the law I became as one under the law (though not being myself under the law) that I might win those under the law. [21] To those outside the law I became as one outside the law

---

[61] Biblical Research Reports, List of Commands in the New Testament, http://www.biblicalresearch reports.com

(not being outside the law of God but under the law of Christ) that I might win those outside the law.

Paul was passionate about winning the lost. He set aside his personal preferences whenever necessary to point others to Christ. When he was with his fellow Jews, he acted as one of them. The Jews' trademark was the Mosaic Law. So to those *"under the law, I became as one under the law."* I can imagine when Paul ate with his countrymen, he ate the food served without claiming his freedom as a Christian. Paul did not open his lunch box and begin eating a pork sandwich. He kept the Law when he was with them.

Paul wanted to clarify his position to those believers In Corinth so he adds, *"though not being myself under the law."* Paul was not trusting in the Law; he was obedient to the law as a tool to reach unbelievers. Paul knew his union with Christ was far greater than the Mosaic Law.

Paul reverses the argument and says that when he is with those not under the Law of Moses (Gentiles) he acts like they do, not being under the restrictions of the Mosaic code. Then Paul includes a powerful statement. Even when he is with those not under the Law of Moses, for Paul, he is still UNDER LAW. **Not the Mosaic Law, but the Law of Christ.**

Galatians 4:1-2

Brothers, if anyone is caught in any transgression, you who are spiritual should restore him in a spirit of gentleness. Keep watch on yourself, lest you too be tempted. [2] Bear one another's burdens, and so fulfill the law of Christ.

We now have the second use of the term "Law of Christ." Paul is not attempting to define it, but to show how bearing one another's burdens fulfills the "Law of Christ." We are to restore family members who are caught in *"any transgression."* Unfortunately, many church laws make it difficult or impossible to restore believers. We are quick to criticize, quick to render judgment and too often withdraw our hand of fellowship instead of reaching out to help. How does this "fulfill the law of Christ?"

In his final words to his disciples, Jesus told them to teach the nations to observe what he commanded them (Matthew 28:20). What did Jesus 'command' us to do?

John 13:34-35

A new commandment I give to you, that you love one another: just as I have loved you, you also are to love one another. [35] By this all people will know that you are my disciples, if you have love for one another."

Why is the commandment to "love one another" new? Was there no commandment to love given before? Charles Leiter in his book the Law of Christ gives three reasons.

1. The new covenant is called "new" because it accompanies a new covenant… This new covenant is not some kind of new legal code or list of rules to be observed, but a reminder of what is really important in the Christian life.

2. It is also "new" because it gives an entirely new depth of meaning to the word love… There can be nothing more exacting, or more demanding, or more wonderful than this, to love others in just the same way and to the same degree that Christ loved us.

3. I John 2:7-8 The Message *"My dear friends, I'm not writing anything new here. This is the oldest commandment in the book, and you've known it from day one. It's always been implicit in the Message you've heard. On the other hand, perhaps it is new, freshly minted as it is in both Christ and you—the darkness on its way out and the True Light already blazing!* Something that is now true "in Christ and in us." As Christians we now belong to a new realm and

a new age, we are new creatures with new hearts and new natures.[62]

Then in the John 15:12 Jesus gives us his commandment.

This is my commandment, that you love one another as I have loved you.

We cannot miss this. Walking in the new covenant is not learning and following hundreds of commandments. It is very simple yet difficult. It is simple to know but difficult to walk out in everyday life. It is so difficult, or can I say impossible, we are given a helper, the Holy Spirit, to live out this commandment through us. The essence of Christian living is loving like Jesus loves us. When we walk this out we also fulfill the moral laws of God, found throughout the Bible.

Jesus narrows the type of love he is talking about. Our love for one another must go beyond anything seen before, it is a new type of love; the love of Christ. How did Christ love us? In Romans 5:8 we are told *"while we were still sinners, Christ died for us."* We have a new standard for love. We are to love in the same manner of Jesus. Even when we were enemies to Jesus, he loved us.

I find it interesting that Paul ends his discussion about fulfilling the Law of Christ by reminding us that being a Jew or Gentile is not the issue; but being a new creation. Those who walk in the rule of no distinctions, Paul prays peace and mercy upon them. He wants God's blessing on these new people of God, those of the new creation—the Israel of God.

> For neither circumcision counts for anything, nor uncircumcision, but a **new creation**. [16] And as for all who walk by this rule, peace and mercy be upon them, and upon the Israel of God (Gal. 4:15).

---

[62] Charles Leiter, The Law of Christ, Granted Ministries Press, 2012, kindle edition.

The "law of Christ" flows from the "new creation." The Laws governing the old creation no longer have authority; they passed away with the old covenant. **The core essence of Christ's Law is love.** When we love others—even those caught in sin—like Christ loves us, we walk in true new covenant life.

Romans 8:2

There is therefore now no condemnation for those who are in Christ Jesus. [2] For the law of the Spirit of life has set you free in Christ Jesus from the law of sin and death.

Although not the exact wording as the previous two, I believe we have here a third reference to the Law of Christ. It is called the "Law of the Spirit" which highlights the power of the Spirit bringing believers into the life of the new covenant. The work of the Spirit brings us to Christ. It is the Spirit which enables us to walk in the Law of Christ.

John 15:17

These things I command you, so that you will love one another.

The instructions and teaching of Jesus had a single goal in mind; that his followers would love one another. Too simple? At first it may seem that way, but as we continue I believe we will see the new covenant is superior to the old because of its simplistic approach. Paul said the same thing to Timothy; "*The aim of our charge is love* (I Tim. 1:5). The Message is good on this passage; "*The whole point of what we're urging is simply love—love uncontaminated by self-interest and counterfeit faith, a life open to God* (The Message I Tim. 1:5-6).

Even though the goal is simple the application is supernatural. True love, the kind of love required in the new covenant is only achieved through the Holy Spirit. The covenant we must abide in goes way past obedience but to a change of heart, a change of character, from which the law of Christ flow.

Matthew 7:12

So whatever you wish that others would do to you, do also to them, for **this is the Law and the Prophets.**

Romans 13:8

Owe no one anything, except to love each other, for the one who loves another has fulfilled the law.

Galatians 5:6

For in Christ Jesus neither circumcision nor uncircumcision counts for anything, but only faith working **through love.**

Galatians 5:13

For the whole law is fulfilled in one word: "You shall love your neighbor as yourself.

James 2:8

You do well when you complete the Royal Rule of the Scriptures: "Love others as you love yourself (The Message).

Matthew 22:36-40

Teacher, which is the great commandment in the Law?" [37] And he said to him, "You shall love the Lord your God with all your heart and with all your soul and with all your mind. [38] This is the great and first commandment. [39] And a second is like it: You shall love your neighbor as yourself. [40] On these two commandments depend **all the Law and the Prophets.**

What is Jesus saying here about the law?

Jonathan Welton:

Here, it is important to note that Jesus did not say, "This is My rule for you." He simply summarized the old covenant in two commandments, which we see by His statement, "On these two commandments depend the whole Law and the Prophets." It is a summary of the old, not a new covenant commandment.

Once we understand that, we can look at John 13:34–35, where Jesus said to His disciples:

A new command I give you: Love one another. As I have loved you, so you must love one another. By this everyone will know that you are my disciples, if you love one another.

His command was not "love your neighbor as yourself" but "love others as I love you." In other words, He was telling them to love others in the same way that He loves them. Jesus loves all people equally, perfectly, and unconditionally. This is the standard, the new command, we are to follow. If we search the word command in the Strong's Concordance, what we will find is that this command is the only command Jesus gave. For example, later in John He said, "My command is this: Love each other as I have loved you" (John 15:12), and, "This is my command: Love each other" (John 15:17).[63]

Charles Leiter: *"Under the old covenant there were all sorts of laws and regulations to be meticulously followed—in fact, six hundred and thirteen of them!* **Under the new covenant, there is only one guidepost for us to keep central in our thinking—to love as Christ loved!***...The emphasis of the New Testament is not on any written list of commandments and prohibitions as our standard of conduct, but on Christian love that is empowered and directed by the Holy Spirit."*[64]

This is the heart of our glorious covenant; to love as Christ loves! This replaces all the rules in the world. We will please God, walk

---

[63] Jonathan Welton, Understanding the Whole Bible, 2014, p. 259
[64] Charles Leiter, The Law of Christ, Granted Ministries Press, Hannibal, Missouri, 2012

in holiness, be a blessing to others, and fulfill every commandment of Jesus.

What is the "Law of Christ?" It can be answered in one word; love. Love as Jesus loves us!

We do not love in any way that feels good, we do not love according to human tradition or the culture of the hour. Our love comes from Christ. Without the Holy Spirit working in our lives we will not achieve this kind of love. Thank God we have the Spirit so we can fulfill the Law of Christ.

Walking in the Law of Christ is key to changing our lives. It will change the church. It will transform the nations. There is no other way. Why return to Moses when we have Christ?

We need no lists of rules, no church saying "if you do this we kick you out" and we need no theology saying we must keep most, some, or a few Old Testament laws, and we need no one saying just keep the 1,050 New Testament laws; we need to walk in love. Period! That's it folks!

The Charge of Antinomianism

When anyone questions the Law of Moses, the charge of 'antinomianism' is heard. "Without God's Law Christians will become lawless and sin without restraint." Is this true? Are those living under grace of the new covenant without law? No, we certainly are not! Christians are not without God's Law! We have the Law of Christ. Christ is superior to Moses and his law is superior. The Law of Christ is the ultimate Law of God. Christ received all authority from his Father; therefore, his law is the authoritative standard for the Church. There is no higher or better law.

Chapter 13

The Glorious Covenant
is Christocentric

No matter what theological system we adopt, all roads must meet at the revelation of Christ. Let this be our compass as we journey towards resolving these difficult areas of Scripture. Understanding the relationship between law and grace, old covenant and new covenant is not easy and with so many interpretations we need a guide. The new covenant begins with the cross. Old Testaments prophets spoke of it, but until Jesus hung on the cross, the new covenant was only a dream.

Israel's Messiah comes in the middle of history and is the apex of history. Any system of biblical interpretation which makes the Incarnation and ministry of Jesus anything less than central is off-center in its approach. The first century was the eschatological fulfillment of everything Israel had been promised. The new covenant is centered in the blood of Jesus. Dispensationalism misses this because it postpones the new covenant until after the Second Coming. Covenant Theology misses the point and makes the new covenant a better administration of what was established by Moses. Moses and Christ cannot be compared, neither can their Laws. New Covenant Theology misses the vital connection of a full-orbed ministry of the Spirit and its connection to eschatology.

Luke 22:20

Likewise also the cup after supper, saying, this cup [is] the new testament in my blood, which is shed for you.

This verse in Luke connects the work of Jesus on the cross to the new covenant. It is a direct statement of fact, not much interpretation needed. Without the cross we remain under the old covenant. The new is available because of the sacrifice of Jesus. Since the cross Jesus is center of all creation. All roads do not lead to God; Jesus does!

Hebrews 8:6-7

> But as it is, Christ has obtained a ministry that is as much more excellent than the old as the covenant he mediates is better, since it is enacted on better promises. [7] For if that first covenant had been faultless, there would have been no occasion to look for a second.

Why has Christ obtained a more excellent ministry than Moses? Hebrews says because it is *"enacted on better promises."* What are these better promises? For old covenant people, God promised blessings, defeat of their enemies, the status of a great people and a land to possess. Reading the Old Testament we become aware of the numerous blessing promised to the people of the Law.

The Better Promises of the New Covenant

First, our sins are forgiven.

Second, we receive the Holy Spirit.

Third, we have the promise for healing in our physical bodies.

Fourth, we have the promise of the resurrection of the dead.

Fifth, we experience God's greater glory.

Sixth, we worship in the New Jerusalem.

Seventh, we are seated in heavenly places.

Eighth, we are saved by grace and walk in grace.

Ninth, we are a new creation.

Tenth, we have eternal redemption.

Eleventh, we have the "Law of Christ."

Twelfth, the nations will be converted and the knowledge of the glory of God will cover the earth.

The list goes on and on. Certainly the promises under the new covenant are far superior to what was given to the people under the old covenant. There is no comparison.

Going back to the discussion between dispensational and covenant theology which breaks over the issue of continuity or discontinuity, it is clear to me that the author of Hebrews stresses discontinuity. He reveals a clear distinction between the old and the new. We have a second covenant and therefore there is no longer a need for the first.

Hebrews 9:11-15

But when Christ appeared as a high priest of the good things that have come, then through the greater and more perfect tent (not made with hands, that is, not of this creation) [12] he entered once for all into the holy places, not by means of the blood of goats and calves but by means of his own blood, thus securing an eternal redemption. [13] For if the blood of goats and bulls, and the sprinkling of defiled persons with the ashes of a heifer, sanctify for the purification of the flesh, [14] how much more will the blood of Christ, who through the eternal Spirit offered himself without blemish to God, purify our conscience from dead works to serve the living God. [15] Therefore he is the mediator of a new covenant, so that those who are called may receive the promised eternal inheritance, since a death has occurred that redeems them from the transgressions committed under the first covenant.

This passage is significant for establishing a theology based upon the glorious and better covenant. First, we must see where Jesus established this new covenant: Was it completed at his death on the cross or were there additional actions needed? Jesus is the mediator of a new covenant based upon his ministry as a high priest.

Therefore, after his death he enters the temple, not the physical temple of the old covenant but the heavenly temple (not of this creation) and offers his blood (not the blood of goats and calves) on the heavenly altar. With this action Jesus secured for us "forgiveness of sins, a pure conscience and an eternal inheritance." So even though the work of the cross was the sacrifice needed to secure our salvation Jesus needed to offer his blood upon the altar of heaven.

Baker's Evangelical Dictionary:

Beginning with Hebrews chapter 5 the central theological concern of the epistle emerges: the eternal spiritual priesthood assumed by Jesus through offering up himself as the once-for-all sacrifice for sins. It is infinitely superior to the temporal earthly ministry exercised by Aaron and his descendants (4:14-5:11; 7:1-10:18).

Here the Christology of Hebrews reaches its loftiest peak as Jesus, the eternal high priest, enters the inner sanctum of the universe where he offers up his own body and blood in voluntary submission to God as a sacrifice for sins once, forever, in behalf of all humanity. He is both priest and victim, offerer and offering![65]

Matthew Easton in writing about the purpose of the book of Hebrews tells us what happened to the Law of Moses once Christ offered himself as the final sacrifice.

Easton's Bible Dictionary (Authored by Matthew George Easton-1823-1894-a Scottish Presbyterian):

Its design was to show the true end and meaning of the Mosaic system, and its symbolical and transient character. It proves that the Levitical priesthood was a "shadow" of that of Christ, and that the legal sacrifices prefigured the great and all-perfect sacrifice he offered for us. It explains that the gospel was designed, not to modify the Law of Moses, but to supersede and abolish it.[66]

---

[65] Baker's Evangelical Dictionary of Biblical Theology, http://biblestudytools.com
[66] Easton's Bible Dictionary, http://biblestudytools.com

I love Easton's phrase **"the gospel was designed, not to modify the Law of Moses, but to supersede and abolish it."** Why would anyone attempt or desire to rebuild what Christ abolished?

The new covenant is greater in every aspect to the old. Jonathan Welton in <u>Understanding the Whole Bible</u> is right on target.

People often get the idea that we cannot keep the Law from James 1, where it says that if we violate one part of the Law we violate it all. In other words, it requires 100 percent consistency. That is true, and that makes the Law difficult, but it does not make it impossible. James and the other apostles argued against returning to the Law, not because it is impossible but because it was an inferior covenant.[67]

Yes the old was inferior. The new is superior because it brings the light of our attention to Jesus. He is the center of all doctrine, the core message of the Bible and the mediator of a new and better covenant. The Mosaic Law can never match what the new covenant offers; Jesus. Moses pointed forward to Jesus but once the reality came, what was once glorious becomes dim in comparison.

With the coming of Jesus a new age opened up. The kingdom of God is established and the new covenant is born; all centered in the work of Jesus. The glorious covenant is Christocentric!

Colossians 1:18

And he is the head of the body, the church. He is the beginning, the firstborn from the dead, that in everything he might be preeminent.

Or, as translated by The Message.

He was supreme in the beginning and—leading the resurrection parade—he is supreme in the end. From beginning to end he's there, towering far above everything, everyone. So spacious is he, so roomy, that everything of

---

[67] Jonathan Welton, Understanding the Whole Bible, 2014, p. 169

God finds its proper place in him without crowding. Not only that, but all the broken and dislocated pieces of the universe—people and things, animals and atoms—get properly fixed and fit together in vibrant harmonies, all because of his death, his blood that poured down from the cross (Col. 18-20).

Chapter 14

The Glorious Covenant
is Creational Eschatology

We now arrive at the point where covenant and eschatology meet. To say "meet" may be overreaching because covenant and eschatology have a long history working in partnership throughout biblical history. The term Creational Eschatology[68] is a newer term but points towards the close relationship of covenant and eschatology. By using 'creational' we are pointing in the direction of a new creation which takes place with the coming of Messiah. With the establishment of a new covenant God through Christ remakes his creation, setting right what has been wrong. God's first step in setting right his world is creating a new people;[69] a new covenant people, and when this happens we have a new understanding of eschatology.

When Paul needed a word to show what happens to those "in Christ" he uses "new creation." This evokes God in the beginning at the first creation. Now he is at work again, creating a new creation. It is not a new physical creation but a renewal of the original. It is spiritual remaking through the work of Christ.

Creational eschatology is an accurate term because the old covenant is symbolized by creation language. When the old heavens and earth give way to new heavens and earth, it is language of covenant. The physical earth remains the same, it is not burned up or destroyed. With Jesus' announcement of the kingdom of God we begin a new age, a new covenant is coming, and it is superior to all that preceded

---

68   NT Wright, Paul and the Faithfulness of God, Fortress Press, Minneapolis, Minnesota, 2013, p. 926
69   Ibid.

it. Not only is it superior but it fulfills all before it; certainly everything is becoming new.

To fully grasp the picture of eschatology and covenant we return to the early history of Israel and see how their eschatology differs from their pagan neighbors. Most nations had their version of eschatology, some, were quite elaborate while others quite simple. The common denominator of pagan nations was the explanation of and preparation for the next life, after death.

Egypt built enormous tombs so their leaders could enjoy the afterlife and have ample provision. Great imagination was released in creating alternative versions of the afterlife. Pagan nations surrounding Israel attempted to explain the afterlife. But Israel was different.

Israel's version of eschatology was about a time in their future when God will make everything right. Their eschatology was not based upon after death theories but about a better life before death. It took hundreds of years before the concept of resurrection was widely accepted. And this resurrection was not the hope of attaining heaven, but coming back to life with all the faithful of Israel in the new age; when Israel's promises from God were to be realized.[70] Their hope was not in another world but that Israel would live at peace and be blessed in their own land.[71]

We learn a great lesson from Israel. With an alarming amount of science fiction eschatology running amuck in the modern church, a strong dose of a hopeful future eschatology for this world would be welcomed by many. Too few Christians center their hope in a renewed world; they only want to escape. Biblical eschatology through Scripture is not speaking about our hope after we die but for

---

[70] N.T. Wright, Paul and the Faithfulness of God, Fortress Press, Minneapolis, Minnesota, 2013, p. 1066

[71] N.T. Wright, Paul and the Faithfulness of God, Fortress Press, Minneapolis, Minnesota, 2013, p. 1044

a better world. It was the pagans who were overly concerned about what happens after death; Israel wanted a better life in this world.

How was this eschatology of hope structured for Israel? It came progressively through divinely given covenants. The revelation of eschatology—their future hope—came by way of covenant. In covenant after covenant God created a picture of what their future would look like if they were faithful. The covenants given to Abraham, David, and Jeremiah were not promises fulfilled in heaven but for this world.

Once we arrive at the New Testament this marriage of eschatology and covenant comes together in Jesus. Jesus is the "hope of Israel." Jesus is their Messiah and upon him rests the entire history of Israel's hope. Now we have a new covenant where all their eschatological hope will be realized.

We have alluded several times as to how our understanding of covenant and kingdom need exegetical and theological agreement. We do ourselves injustice to think one pulls the other off center. If we distort our view of kingdom (like dispensationalism and their 1,000 year millennium) or ignore eschatology in our covenant understanding (NCT) then our concept of covenant becomes distorted as well. The best way to connect the two realities of covenant and kingdom is to say the kingdom of God comes to us through the new covenant. The kingdom does not flow through the old covenant.

Think of covenant like a computer. All computers have an operating system. The people in the Old Testament used the Mosaic Law as their operating system. Once Jesus came, he introduced a completely new system, the new covenant. If we attempt to live as Christians and resort back to the old operating system, we miss out on the power and higher functioning new system. The new covenant is far superior to what the people of the Old Testament operated under.

D.A. Carson, when discussing Matthew 5:17, states correctly the role of Jesus:

Jesus *"presents himself as the eschatological goal of the OT, and thereby its sole authoritative interpreter, the one through whom alone the OT finds its valid continuity and significance."*[72]

Jesus arrives in history during the eschatological last days of Israel signifying that the old covenant of Israel is about to be re-defined by Jesus. He is the lone source of authority. The leaders of Israel are about to meet the one who has the final word on everything pertaining to the old covenant.

Noah, Abraham, and David were not entirely faithful to their covenant. Each had issues and sin. Jesus is the one and only true faithful covenant partner. Paul says *"all the promises of God find their Yes in him* (II Cor. 1:20).

The Old Testament covenants took several thousand years to bring us to Jesus. Each covenant added to our body of knowledge as what should be expected. When Jesus walks onto the stage of history there is a large body of prophecies and promises which become the foundation for his kingdom work.

Gentry and Wellum:

"From what has been started, it should be fairly evident how we think kingdom and covenant are conjoined. It is primarily through the biblical covenants viewed diachronically that we learn how the saving reign of God comes to this world. In other words, the relationship between the kingdom of God and the biblical covenants is a tight one, and it is at the heart of understanding how God's kingdom dawns in Jesus."[73]

---

[72] D.A. Carson, Matthew Vol.1, The Expositor's Bible Commentary by D. A. Carson, Frank E. Gaebelein and J. D. Douglas, Zondervan, 1995, **p. 144**
[73] Peter J. Gentry, Stephen J. Wellum, Kingdom through Covenant, Crossway, Wheaton, Illinois, 2012, p. 601

I'm glad to see New Covenant Theology associating covenant with kingdom. I just wish they would take the additional step and identify the kingdom of God with eschatology, which a majority of NCT authors have not done. Since many in the NCT camp have a Baptist tradition, separating from Premillennialism is a major step and one which may not set well within their institutions and fellowships. Time is on their side and hopefully, they will eventually see how a revelation of the new covenant is linked to the present and advancing kingdom.

My reason for insisting eschatology—or kingdom—must be studied in union with covenant is because it is through the kingdom language of Jesus we learn of the coming new covenant. Jesus opening his ministry with the words "The kingdom of God is at hand," not "The new covenant is at hand." Jesus used the one concept all first century Jews would recognize. Even though Isaiah spoke of a future covenant two hundred years before Jeremiah did, the hope of God coming and fulfilling all his promises was perfectly contained in the language of the kingdom being at hand. Astute Jews knowing their Scripture, may also have connected this arrival with Jeremiah's new covenant. Even if it was lost in the opening excitement it was not too long before Jesus connected his soon coming death with the new covenant.

The words "creational eschatology" hopefully now have more meaning. A new time for Israel is opening, their Messiah is here, teaching, healing, and proclaiming the age of the kingdom. Since Jesus is announcing such radical change, the old creation with its old covenant is surely coming to an end. With the kingdom we receive the glorious promises and with the new covenant we receive the relationship with God through the Messiah in order to experience these divine and magnificent promises. One flows into the other. Jesus first announces the coming of the kingdom and then later explains the sacrifice it takes to open up this new world. There will be no kingdom for those unwilling to enter the new covenant. Israel or Gentiles have one choice: if you want the kingdom, accept the terms of the new covenant.

From the practical side of creational eschatology I believe new covenant believers ought to be among the most creative people in society. We are born again from above with a desire to create, to express what has never been seen or heard before. In areas of music, art, architecture, environment, business, education, entertainment, law and justice, and engineering, just to name a few, Christians are to lead the way. This is the challenge of the coming generations. I am committed to developing new thinking in biblical theology, not as an end in itself, but as impetuous to encourage taking our faith to our culture.

Chapter 15

The Glorious Covenant is Glorious

The old covenant with its extensive laws is not an end-all in God's desire for a holy people; it is only the first step. We now have the substance which the shadow intended to convey. *"For since the law has but a shadow of the good things to come* (Hebrews 10:1).

We cannot remain in the shadows. There are too many "good things" available to us. Christians walking around in shadows will fail to see the true light of Christ. Shadow Christians tend to be judgmental, simplistic and overly confident in their shadowy doctrines.

Apostle Paul in his letter to the believers in Corinth writes about the new covenant.

II Corinthians 3:3

And you show that you are a letter from Christ delivered by us, written not with ink but with the Spirit of the living God, not on tablets of stone but on tablets of human hearts.

He alludes to the Law written on stone tablets and given to Moses. Now, the Holy Spirit replaces previous forms of writing to write on *"human hearts."*

Paul continues:

Such is the confidence that we have through Christ toward God. [5] Not that we are sufficient in ourselves to claim anything as coming from us, but our sufficiency is from God, [6] who has made us sufficient to be ministers of a new covenant, not of the letter but of the Spirit. For the letter kills, but the Spirit gives life (verses 4-6).

Paul is clear, he is not a Jew attempting to make Gentiles follow the Mosaic Law. God made Apostle Paul a minister of the "new covenant." His statement *"The letter kills"* must be seen in context, he is speaking of the old covenant. He does not desire any confusion on the matter; the old covenant brings forth death but the Spirit of the new covenant gives life.

Glory to Glory

> Now if the ministry of death, carved in letters on stone, came with such glory that the Israelites could not gaze at Moses' face because of its glory, which was being brought to an end, [8] will not the ministry of the Spirit have even more glory? [9] For if there was glory in the ministry of condemnation, the ministry of righteousness must far exceed it in glory. [10] Indeed, in this case, **what once had glory has come to have no glory at all,** because of the glory that surpasses it. [11] For if what was being brought to an end came with glory, much more will what is permanent have glory (Verses 7-11).

Even the old covenant had glory. No one denies that. Whatever God does, wherever he speaks, when he performs miracles, it carries aspects of his person, his character. So when Moses receives the old covenant it came with the glory of God. What about now? Does Moses and his covenant contain any glory? Does it still carry the authority of God? No! Paul says, *"What once had glory has come to have no glory at all."* It is sad when Evangelical believers attempt to squeeze out glory from the old covenant when according to Paul, there is none. It is time to stop a lot of foolishness; stop blowing shofars thinking they have a special anointing. Stop parading around the Israeli flag believing you are standing with God's chosen people. Stop pretending you are the bloodline of Abraham if you are not. Stop dressing like Jews from the Middle Ages. Stop using Jewish prayer shawls. Why? Because in Christ we stop pretending and become true recipients of Abraham and his promises. It comes through the new covenant, not trying to revive the old. Get out of the shadows, the substance is much better.

When Jesus died on the cross the veil of the temple was torn. This was a sign that Israel's God had a new system of worship; the old temple had no authority. Jesus told them earlier in Matthew 23 about their temple; it would be left desolate (Matt. 23:38). The old covenant lost its authority at the cross. Yet, the outward system remained until 70 AD when the Romans destroyed the temple and city. There was a generation between the time of its official ending and its visible ending. Once the temple was destroyed Christianity and Judaism were no longer seen as belonging to each other. Judaism was now a dead religion. Judaism is still dead. It has no living covenant with God.

Since I believe this is what the Bible teaches I must adjust my doctrine of modern Israel. Even if I support Israel as a political nation I cannot use the Bible for my support. Also, since many Jews living in Israel are the children of Gentiles who converted to Judaism in the seventh century, it becomes problematic to see them as direct descendants of Abraham. No one knows for sure. Also, all official records were destroyed in the burning of the temple in 70 AD. This is a difficult issue, especially since emotion often rules the discussion. One group's research is quickly rebuffed by a different group, so the debate continues. Even with this said here are a few enlightening quotes:

The Jewish Encyclopedia:
"Khazars, a non-Semitic, Asiatic, Mongolian tribal nation who emigrated into Eastern Europe about the first century, who were converted as an entire nation to Judaism in the seventh century by the expanding Russian nation which absorbed the entire Khazar population, and who account for the presence in Eastern Europe of the great numbers of Yiddish-speaking Jews in Russia, Poland, Lithuania, Galatia, Besserabia and Rumania."

The American Peoples Encyclopedia: *"In the year 740 A.D. the Khazars were officially converted to Judaism. A century later they were crushed by the incoming Slavic-speaking people and were scattered over central Europe where they were known as Jews."*[74]

Encyclopedia Britannica (15th edition):

"Khazars, confederation of Turkic and Iranian tribes that established a major commercial empire in the second half of the 6th century, covering the southeastern section of modern European Russia... In the middle of the 8th century the ruling classes adopted Judaism as their religion."

How can a Gentile convert to a covenant which has been dead for 700 years? This is what the Khazars did; they converted to Judaism. Sure, anyone can convert and join a religion, there are many religions. Even if all modern Jews are direct descendants of Abraham, it still does not mean they have a covenant with God. Their covenant ended. Their covenant is now desolate; it has no spiritual authority. The house and covenant of old Israel is left empty.

With this in mind how can unsaved Gentiles inherit the promises to Abraham? If the majority of Jews are descendants of the Khazars are they not still Gentiles in the eyes of God (if God is concerned about such distinctions). And when they come to Christ all such distinctions are dissolved anyway (Eph.2:11-17, Gal. 3:28).

The Christian Zionist position that Israel is the chosen people of God stands on thin biblical ice. It is not supported by Jesus or the rest of the New Testament. Yet for many reason it gathers great support from Evangelical Christians. This undermines the church; it robs the church of its rightful blessings and takes away any incentive to evangelize particular nations like Israel. Let us unite together and

---

[74]   Social-Economics History Blog, http://Socioecohistory.wordpress.com

defeat this insane replacement theology which steals the promises for the church and gives them to the nation of Israel.[75]

Matthew 23:37-38

"O Jerusalem, Jerusalem, the city that kills the prophets and stones those who are sent to it! How often would I have gathered your children together as a hen gathers her brood under her wings, and you were not willing! [38] See, your house is left to you desolate."

We are still speaking of how the glory of the past covenant cannot be compared with the new covenant. The past is no longer with us. With Jesus we are under a new, living and glorious covenant.

Paul writes:

But when one turns to the Lord, the veil is removed. [17] Now the Lord is the Spirit, and where the Spirit of the Lord is, there is freedom. [18] And we all, with unveiled face, beholding the glory of the Lord, are being transformed into the same image from one degree of glory to another. For this comes from the Lord who is the Spirit (II Cor. 3; 16-18).

The glorious covenant carries more glory than the old covenant because the glory is **ever-increasing**! The old covenant was temporary and so was its glory. We now live with a glory which never departs. And, a glory which is ever increasing in our lives. If we desire better experiences and revelation of truth under the new covenant, then seek a greater filling of the Spirit. Walking with the Holy Spirit in the new covenant should never be routine. The depths of God discovered through the Spirit is never ending. Every time we hear the word of God taught, every worship service, time in prayer,

---

[75] For those not following the theological debate on 'replacement theology' I am using the phrase in reverse for making my point. Normally 'replacement theology' means the theology of taking the promises to Israel and assigning them to the church.

and fellowship with the saints, it gives opportunity to experience the ever-increasing glory in our lives.

It bewilders me why people of Pentecostal/Charismatic experience support Dispensationalism with its emphasis upon returning to Old Testament law and its lack of emphasis upon the work of the Spirit. The Holy Spirit provides us freedom, liberty, and the ability to walk in the fullness of the new covenant. The Holy Spirit and the connection with the life-giving new covenant cannot be overlooked.

Paul was right, the covenant we have is more glorious than any previous covenant. Thank God for sending his son, thank God we live in a Glorious Covenant; the better covenant.

Final Score: Four Positions of Covenant

1. Dispensational Theology

2. Covenant Theology

3. New Covenant Theology

4. Better Covenant Theology

First, we saw Dispensationalism fall in a head to head match with Covenant Theology. Then Covenant Theology moved to the next round and lost badly to New Covenant Theology. Our final match saw New Covenant Theology take on the Better Covenant Theology. Who wins? I made my case, it is up to you. I am convinced what is briefly outlined moves us closer to what the New Testament teaches. New Covenant Theology gives us a number of quality points which are superior to the first two, but it has its faults as we outlined. This is only the beginning to develop a fourth way of thinking. I believe "Better Covenant Theology" over time offers the church a true theological alternative and adheres to what the New Testament teaches. By God's grace we will see Scripture deeper and clearer. A true fourth alternative will emerge and the people of God free to advance the kingdom.

These are our four choices. My opinion on which best represents the teaching of the New Testament can be seen if we reverse the order of our list.

1. **Better Covenant Theology**

2. New Covenant Theology

3. Covenant Theology

4. Dispensational Theology

Section Three –
Glorious Covenant in Practice

Chapter 16

Practical Considerations

(Subjects provoking Controversy)

How does our view of the new covenant help in practical areas? What is new covenant living? When we get to the practical side of theology emotions kick into high gear and everyone has opinions. The average church person may not be comfortable discussing Covenant Theology but when it comes to tattoos, drinking alcohol, money, abusive leaders, clothes, and a host of issues, we all become world-renown scholars and theologians. We will address a few areas and see how understanding the new covenant helps in bringing biblical sanity back into the discussion. Although there are many issues we will briefly review five areas: curses, the tithe, clothing and dress, drinking alcohol, and abusive leaders.

1. Curses

Getting free from curses is popular nowadays especially among Charismatics. Leaders even use curses to raise money, demand obedience and all sorts of devious things. If you can convince a person they are cursed for certain failures; then nothing is off the table. There are church leaders who pronounce curses over people if they leave their church. People are cursed if they miss a tithe payment. The list is long. Then we have numerous believers standing in prayer lines to be released from curses. Curses are real, they are based upon Scripture. Here is a sample of some old covenant curses.

Deuteronomy 27:15-19

[15]Cursed be the man who makes a carved or cast metal image, an abomination to the LORD, a thing made by the hands of a craftsman, and sets it up in secret. [16] Cursed be anyone who dishonors his father or his mother. [17] Cursed be anyone who moves his neighbor's landmark. [18] Cursed be anyone who misleads a blind man on the road. [19] Cursed be anyone who perverts the justice due to the sojourner, the fatherless, and the widow.

In verse 26 we have the curse of curses, anyone breaking the Law of Moses is under a curse.

Cursed be anyone who does not confirm the words of this law by doing them (26).

Keeping the Law of Moses was serious. No one was allowed to choose certain laws to obey and ignore the rest; all the law was kept or you came under a curse.

From Bakers Evangelical Dictionary:

"Nowhere in the Bible is the state of being cursed portrayed in more graphic terms than in Deuteronomy 28:16-68. The curse follows its victims everywhere, extending to progeny and all means of livelihood. It includes incurable diseases, slow starvation, abuse by enemies, exile, panic, confusion, and eventual madness."[76]

Being cursed for breaking the Law of Moses carried severe consequences. **You may get incurable diseases, starve to death, be exiled, and even go insane**. This is not a religion one is to take lightly. The big question we must ask; do the curses found in the Law of Moses carry over to the new covenant? Should Christians be afraid of curses?

---

[76]   Bakers Evangelical Dictionary of Biblical Theology, From http://biblestudytools,com

Romans 12:14

Bless those who persecute you; bless and do not curse them.

Even when our enemies attack us, we are not to curse them. Paul understood the old covenant power of a curse and did not want Christians engaged is such activities. Christian relationships with unbelievers is based upon wanting their salvation not their destruction. We bless them because we desire they know the love of God.

James 3:10

From the same mouth come blessing and cursing. My brothers, these things ought not to be so.

James feels believers should not be the source of both cursing and blessings. We are to be a single fountain; flowing from the Holy Spirit who fills us.

I John 5:18

We know that everyone who has been born of God does not keep on sinning, but he who was born of God protects him, and the evil one does not touch him.

Can Apostle John be clearer? Those "*born of God*" the "*evil one does not touch him.*" As Christians we live in the light. If you live in or walk near darkness then expect to meet spirits who live in darkness. The answer is to stay away from darkness. The exception is when we are ministering to those living in darkness and in those situations we are to remember Jesus overcame the world and gave us the victory.

Galatians 3:13

Christ redeemed us from the curse of the law by becoming a curse for us—for it is written, "Cursed is everyone who is hanged on a tree"

Old Testament curses came from God. It was in response to their disobedience. In the new covenant we are free from these type of curses.

Romans 7:6

But now we are released from the law, having died to that which held us captive, so that we serve in the new way of the Spirit and not in the old way of the written code.

This verse in the book of Romans is good news for new covenant believers. We have been released from the Law of Moses. Under no circumstance place yourself back under the old covenant law. We have died to the law by our union with Christ.

Jeremiah 31:29-31

In those days they shall no longer say: "'The fathers have eaten sour grapes, and the children's teeth are set on edge." ^{30} But everyone shall die for his own iniquity. Each man who eats sour grapes, his teeth shall be set on edge. ^{31} "Behold, the days are coming," declares the LORD, "when I will make a new covenant with the house of Israel and the house of Judah."

I have avoided Old Testament Scriptures in favor of New Testament ones because it reveals the greater light. Yet, this passage in Jeremiah shows how curses work under the new covenant. The statement about a father eating sour grapes and the children's teeth being set on edge is an old Hebrew proverb. It meant the sins of the father will be passed down to the children. This was the case under the old covenant. What does Jeremiah says about this principle? Something will change and *everyone shall die for his own iniquity.* This is followed by a prophecy of the new covenant. Under the new covenant these types of generation curses are not allowed. I do not think that what is taught in many churches about generation curses remains under the new covenant. Once again, we see a mixture of old and new; the result is confusion, guilt and manipulation.

We live under the new covenant. The rules of the old covenant no longer apply. Read the words of the New Testament, allow the Spirit to help you understand. All 613 Laws of Moses have served their purpose. They are now part of history. The cross of Jesus made sure of it. The destruction of the temple ended all visible sight of the old covenant. According to Hebrews 8:13 the first (old) covenant is *"Becoming obsolete and growing old is ready to vanish away."* Between the cross and 70AD the old covenant was 'growing old." Once the temple burned and was Jerusalem destroyed it vanished. What God caused to disappear let no one attempt to make visible again.

New Covenant Curse

We do find what may be called a new covenant curse in Galatians 1:8 and I Corinthians 16:22.

Galatians 1:8

But even if we or an angel from heaven should preach to you a gospel contrary to the one we preached to you, let him be accursed (anathema).

I Corinthians 16:22

If anyone has no love for the Lord, let him be accursed (anathema).

Bakers Evangelical Dictionary:

"Thus *anathema* in the New Testament became equivalent to *herem* (see footnote) [77]in the Old Testament. This curse was imposed for

---

[77] According to Rabbi Louis Jacobs published by Oxford University Press, *Herem* is a ban imposed on an individual to separate him from the other members of the community. When Joshua destroyed the city of Jericho, he pronounced a herem on anything appertaining to the city and when Achan took of that which was proscribed he was severely punished for his disobedience of the ban.

apostasy (Gal 1:8), not loving Christ (1 Cor. 16:22), and not extending loving care to the least of the brethren (Matt 25:41)."[78]

We will deal with Paul's words in Galatians first. Paul wants those preaching a different gospel to be "accursed." This means they must be separated from the church and have God's judgment upon them. Pronouncing a new covenant curse on people is not a game for preachers with low self-esteem issues. This is not something we pronounce on anyone disagreeing with our doctrine. My view is that this was done in accordance with Paul's apostolic authority, as the primary person writing the doctrines of the Christian faith. It was absolutely necessary Paul keep the gospel pure and not allow any changes or alterations.

Is there another question we can ask? Paul was giving a warning to those attempting to pull the church into false doctrine. No individual was mentioned—or did he say God will bring upon this people the same judgment as those breaking the Law of Moses? I am unsure if this becomes an example of modern church discipline. Any leader who thinks they can function as Paul did, must proceed with caution. We must never forget we are under grace and our understanding of the gospel is growing as we mature in the handling of Scripture.

I Corinthians 16 is a different case. Those who have *"no love for the Lord, let him be accursed."* Who was Paul mad at? I am not sure if he was voicing his anger at anyone as much as detesting the church which had a mixed membership. His words in context are to the church in Corinth. If a person in the church showed no love for the Savior, then in Paul's mind, they were not really part of the church and were there under false pretensions and probably had devious intentions. For people who sneak into local churches with no true heart for God and only want to disrupt things, Paul wants them to be *"accursed."*

---

[78]   Bakers Evangelical Dictionary of Biblical Theology, From http://biblestudytools,com

Conclusion

Do Christians under the new covenant deal with real curses? I see no Scripture evidence for answering yes. In both cases where Paul wanted people cursed they were not genuine believers. With all that said we cannot overlook medical conditions which affect behavior and moods. Also there are emotional ties and wounds from parents which can have strong influence in our lives. These ties can lead to real bondages. I see in these situations people needing healing more than the breaking of a curse

I know there are many in the church who have been healed through breaking curses off their lives. When people get free, we all must rejoice. Prayer for people in the name of Jesus is powerful. Were these people in bondage because they were under an Old Testament type curse? Scripturally, I say no, but we must recognize their hurt and minister the love and power of the risen Christ so they can live free.

2. The 10% Tithe

There is nothing more sacred in our modern western church than the 10% tithe. Threats of all kinds are spoken over those not in compliance. Gross manipulation of believers is an everyday occurrence. This is especially seen on television but local churches are not exempt. Giving or "sowing" money is now seen as the highest method for achieving all types of spiritual victory. If you need healing then give an offering in the exact amount the preacher tells you to. If you want your mortgage paid give a large sum to the traveling evangelist. If you are broke, gather all the money that is left and give an offering—even borrow without means to replay. The list goes on and on. It is sickening how these activities continue.

As in every abuse there is abuse on the other side. The thinking goes like this. We are free. We are free of anyone telling us what to do, no authority in our lives—no pastor and no ministers to take our money. We give as the Holy Spirit leads. Yet, within this new freedom we see Christians spending on lavish entertainment, dinners, vacations, clothes; whatever they desire while giving little or nothing to advance the kingdom of God. None of these things are wrong in themselves. Only when the heart is in the wrong place and we use freedom to excuse selfishness do the activities become troublesome. "The tithe is old covenant" is their cry; yet as far as their giving goes there is little regard for the hardworking pastor, needs of the local church, traveling ministry, missionaries, or caring for the poor. Somehow their freedom allows them to disregard giving entirely.

Both examples are the extreme; but they are not rare. Where is the balance? Where does the teaching of the New Testament take us in relation to our possessions and money? What or whom are we to support with our finances?

Old Testament Tithe

What is the tithe under the old covenant? Giving 10% was not the complete picture; they were required to give much more.

First Tithe: Ten percent was to be given every year except the seventh year. This tithe was for the priests and called the Levite Tithe. What did they tithe? They were to bring cattle, livestock, grains, fruit and vegetables.

Second Tithe: Ten percent was to be given every year except the seventh year (same amount of the Levite Tithe). The same agricultural crops were given. What was the purpose of this tithe? It was to have a celebration at the temple and have a fun vacation. Also, part of the tithe went to the poor so they also could enjoy and celebrate.

Third Tithe: Ten percent were to be given every third year. This is the Charity Tithe. The same produce and livestock were distributed among the Levites, the fatherless, the widows, strangers, and the poor.

When the tithes are added up it comes to 23.33 percent. But when you take out the seventh year the average is right at 20% a year. I'm not aware of any church which asks for 20%, although there have been occasions when a building program was in progress, pastors did ask for a double tithe.

The tithes under the old covenant were to ensure the blessings of God and turn away the wrath of God. It kept the Levites employed and the poor taken care of. Since Israel was more than a religion but also a civil state, these types of tithes were necessary.

A Discussion on Tithing

In a private Facebook group there was a great conversation on Tithing and the new covenant. I received permission to share their thoughts. This is but a few of the comments and as you will see, the subject of tithing evokes strong emotions. I share these comments not because I agree or disagree with each comment, but because it shows why this subject must be discussed openly. We need better answers and biblical teaching on this subject.

Shane Mason

If we are to be completely honest, tithing in the New Covenant scripture is vague and the writers concerning the tithe are mostly quiet. Hence it is quite obvious that tithing is not a "big topic" in the New Testament writings. Honestly, tithing is not mentioned very much in the New Covenant period...HOWEVER, it is a practice "not condemned" either. In all honesty, there is more written pro tithing in The New Covenant, even as slim as that margin is, than there is against it e.g. Matt 23:23; Luke 18:9-14; Heb. 7:1-10...Truthfully there is NOTHING at all written in the New Covenant against the practice of the tithe, though the writers out-rightly condemned other Old Covenant practices. For example we find Paul boldly proclaiming that the Gentiles should not have the burden of circumcision placed upon them!

Yet TODAY, we have people coming out of the woodwork writing and preaching to condemn the practice of New Covenant tithing (something neither Jesus nor His apostles did). They do this even though the "tithe" itself biblically predates the law by some 400 years, and when properly understood related to the throne of David is an obvious principle that is Kingdom by its very nature. (cf. Melchizedek, A Typology of Messiah and Messiah's Kingdom).

To outright condemn tithing seems quite unfair, biased, and intolerant to say the least. It is also contrary to the very nature of the teachings of Christ, Paul and the other apostles. If Jesus and Paul at least acknowledged tithing in a positive light in passing, then what gives us the right to write entire books either dismissing it, or condemning the practice altogether?

Cassandra Beasley-Burton

We thought God would kill us (that's what we were taught) and take His hands off our children if we did not tithe. Then we lost our home because I lost my job and we had to choose between the tithe and paying our mortgage. My husband still does not understand why God did not honor our giving although we were giving in ignorance of the new covenant. I told him I believe it is because, although we absolutely love to give, we were giving thinking this is why God was protecting us and was a prerequisite to Him blessing us, not because He loves us. Then, when we were conflicted about paying bills and shut off notices or paying the "tithe bill to God," we gave, not from the heart but because we HAD to and it was very "begrudgingly." I was so angry at one point with God that I gave my tithe the day we were going to court for foreclosure and I told God at least you have your protection money and rolled my eyes. So glad He is so merciful! Yikes! Just being honest. It really bothers me when people try to say it is not required, but then there is an underlying guilt that is placed out there that says now you can give Him more! What if I have nothing? Just tell me listen to the Holy Spirit and He will show you what and how to give.

I believe because so many have been burned in the church by the obligatory tithe teaching, I would be hesitant to even use the word when it comes to ministering, preaching, and teaching those who have come out of this type of bondage. I was so afraid my children were going to be given over to Satan because we weren't able to do the 10% as this is what we were told. People will need the chance to be healed and taught before I would even use the word, which has become a symbol of abuse and manipulation to so many.

Jonathan Brenneman

Cassandra Beasley-Burton, I had a very similar experience to yours. I have come to believe that the tithing doctrine is one of the greatest assaults on the truth of the gospel that is around. The vast majority of tithe teaching ends up undermining the whole gospel message and in a very subtle and deceptive way teaching salvation by a way other than through Christ. There are so many objections to and problems with teaching the tithe today, any one of which totally destroys it, that I am shocked that so many people have fallen for it. It takes too long to even go into all of the problems and leaps in logic used to defend it. I have seen people manifest demons when it was questioned, and I think that it takes a demonic deception to get a person to keep holding on to it.

Joe McIntyre

I refuse to sit under ministries that use that kind of financial manipulation because I assume the defilement will bleed over into all they teach. We wonder why Evangelicals roll their eyes at Charismatics! When I see them on Christian TV (which I don't watch much of) I immediately turn off certain ones who use these tactics.

Chalet Smith

Many tithe out of obligation because they think it's a mandatory law that redeems them from a financial curse. This is works-based, old covenant theology. The good news is ... in the New Covenant, the curse has already been removed, not because of what you've given the Lord, but because of what He's given you. The NEW COVENANT version of the tithe is GENEROSITY, and there is no more obligation involved ... You're now FREE from the curse of the law ... even if you choose not to give. But understanding this freedom means you are likely to give MORE than ever before.

Brian Davis

And the colossal tithe/curse scripture in Malachi LITERALLY related to food, or "meat" in my house, so the Levite Priesthood could eat, as they were taken care of by this practice, under the law. So the tithe could be considered as a sacrifice for their service. It was however, not money. Now, under a grace covenant, all outward sacrifices cease and we are all spiritual priests who give of our increase according to our hearts, not obligation or need. The law confuses me. I like grace.

Shane Mason

There is some evidence for tithing in New Covenant, Absolutely none about not tithing in the New Covenant. I think we can become religious in not tithing as much as we can in tithing.

Jonathan Brenneman

A practice pre-dating the law doesn't make it not law—you say it biblically pre-dates the law by over 400 years.-So does circumcision, but the NT still teaches that requiring circumcision is holding to the Old Covenant law. There is a stronger basis for circumcision not being law, because at least it was commanded before the law for those who wanted to be in covenant with God, unlike a one-time record 400 years before the law that we have of someone tithing once on spoils of war. Animal sacrifice was also at least commanded before the law; Jesus "mentioned it in a positive light" (according to the same logic that says he was mentioning tithing in a positive light)

The NT repeatedly condemns seeking to relate to God through the law, so therefore teaching tithing is condemned fiercely and repeatedly throughout the NT, along with the other aspects of the law. It didn't need to be condemned specifically like circumcision because it wasn't even an issue. It was, as Jesus said, a minor issue even of the law, not like circumcision which was a big issue for many people and which there were serious disputes about. What about the only thing that is of any value being faith working through love? What about love being the fulfillment of the law?

Of course, with the command that giving be as each person decides in is heart and not under compulsion, the teaching of tithing is also clearly condemned, since it obviously defies this command.

Joe McIntyre

I tell people, "No, you are not limited to 10% in your giving." We are redeemed from the curse of the Law but not the blessing. The blessing of the law was not actually the blessing of the law but it was the blessing of Abraham. Christ has redeemed us from the curse of the law that the blessing of Abraham might come on the Gentiles through faith. Sowing and reaping are eternal laws as long as the earth remains. I tithe and expect Father to richly bless me. I also give Spirit-led gifts as Father leads me. A legalistic approach in my opinion hinders the blessing. Paul speaks of the grace of giving and sowing and reaping in 2 Cor. 8 & 9.

There is no condemnation In Christ: period. Father isn't judging our behavior, He already judged Christ's behavior as sufficient to bring us into a new righteous creation. Our behavior—which realm we sow into—does affect the level of blessing we walk in. As we follow the leading of the indwelling Holy Spirit He leads us to do many things and they bring blessing and increase into our lives.

Jonathan Brenneman

I see the tithing issue today as parallel to the circumcision issue in Galatians, and all of the warnings in Galatians about requiring or even valuing circumcision are just as applicable to the tithing issue. Tithing has no value, the only thing that counts is faith working through love.

I disagree with the statement that the NT never condemned tithing. It expressly tells us that giving must not be under compulsion, and you can't say that there is a 10 percent standard without compelling people. I usually heard it taught that the tithe wasn't giving but a due, like a tax; they used this argument to get around that scripture, but it doesn't work either. Jesus said that the sons of the kingdom were exempt from a temple tax. There is no kingdom of heaven tax. So what are we saying when a person is required to tithe to be a church member, that instead of entering through Christ you enter through the tithe, and it quickly goes from something that it implied to something that is believed explicitly. I am shocked at the extent it has become an explicit teaching.

Acts 15 is pretty clear. The Apostles decided that, of the law, they would only ask the gentile believers to abstain from sexual immorality, from blood, and from things sacrificed to idols. Anything more, they considered to be testing God and putting a burden on the backs of the disciples that neither we nor our ancestors have been able to bear. Yes, the New Testament does condemn the teaching of tithing.

Joe McIntyre

While I think the tithe can certainly be taught legalistically I think some are overreacting to abuses and failing to realize that the laws of sowing and reaping are keys to financial increase according to 2 Cor. 8 & 9. I teach that we are not limited to 10% under the new covenant; we are free to give much more! And God promises to bless our giving when it is given in faith and a response to the Spirit of God. I tithe, but not in legalism, but to honor God with the first fruits of my increase. My church tithes too many other ministries and we claim the blessing of God as we do it. We are delighted to be able to give to ministries that are affecting the world.

I believe in what I would call a grace tithe. Because I knew that Christ had redeemed me from the curse of the law—including the curse for not tithing—that was not an issue personally or in my teaching. But, since all the promises of God are yes and amen in Christ, and there is a promise to the tither of abundance and a rebuking of the devourer, I am free to tithe and claim the promise attached to it without any fear of the curse. When Paul wrote about all the promises he was referring to OT promises because those were the only ones in writing at the time. Peter said we can escape the corruption that is in the world and partake of the divine nature through the promises of God. Every divine promise is an invitation to blessing as far as I'm concerned!

It is the heart of faith that releases God's blessing, not adherence to the law. I fully understand why people are against legalistic tithing. Like many, I started tithing in a legalistic manner. But when I got a revelation of the grace of giving and saw that God would bless my cheerful giving not out of compulsion, I began to see Him bless my giving supernaturally. When God made it real to me that I wasn't under the law as to the tithe, I didn't stop tithing, I just changed the heart of my giving. I know and understand that many teach tithing in a legalistic condemning and manipulative manner and I don't see how God could bless that type of giving. But I still find starting my giving at 10% a good place to begin."

(End of Discussion)

As we can tell from the previous conversation, there is no universal agreement on tithing, even among those of us teaching new covenant living. As cases of manipulation decrease and gathering money through guilt ceases, we may come to agreement on giving. Until then, those abused need healing. And those teaching tithing must base it on the teaching of Jesus and the grace given us under the new covenant. Debating if we should tithe or not, for me, is missing a key point; do we generously and joyfully give to advance the kingdom of God in the earth? If you do not; why not? If you give because you feel guilty; get free! Even if you disagree with the 10% rule the concept of giving God the first fruits is the best way to approach it.

The needs around the world are great. With millions needing to hear the good news of Jesus and his kingdom the debate in time will move from our interpretation of tithing to (hopefully) discussing how we can give more effectively. When we find ministers and local churches working to advance the kingdom, we then can give freely without being forced. We all need to find places to support which mirror our convictions. I think far too many Christians give out of wrong obligation or plain old traditions. I will no longer give where the vision works against my understanding of God's kingdom in the earth. We need a renewal in how believers give their money and where it can best serve the kingdom.

If pastors and church leaders want members to give 10% then the church should lead by example and also give away 10%. The American church in 1920 gave 10% to world missions; the latest numbers show it is 2%.[79] What does the average church do with its 98%? There is no easy answer; many are doing marvelous things and are to be applauded, others spend almost everything to keep themselves spiritually entertained and to maintain the status quo. If we hold a 10% standard or give freely under grace, the challenge is for everyone to help fund taking the gospel of Jesus and his kingdom to all nations. The final words of Jesus was *"Go therefore and make disciples of all nations* (Matthew 28:19).

3. Clothing and Dress

Since clothing is the first thing we normally notice about people I guess it is inevitable it becomes a point of contention in the church. I remember hearing a Baptist pastor years ago admit to his struggle when some leaders in his congregation wanted permission to wear dress shirts—with ties of course—other than standard white. After much soul searching and wrenching of heart the Pastor allowed colored shirts for the Wednesday and Sunday night service but white shirts only must continue for the Sunday morning service. His reluctance was the fear his church would join those Christians who were lowering their standards and becoming too worldly. Today this seems silly yet we have our own versions of the same.

When I was a student in Bible School we had strict rules about clothes. For men, shirts with a tie were mandatory for dinner. This was not presented as a right versus wrong contrast; they were just preparing us to be proper ministers. When it came to wearing jeans,

---

[79]   Generous Giving Research Library, http:/library.generousgiving.org

another reason was given. Jeans in those days were the official dress of the hippie movement, which according to the rule makers, was a sign of rebellion. Wearing jeans was identifying with the sin of rebellion; therefore wearing jeans was not allowed. In my opinion their argument broke down when wearing jeans was allowed on Saturdays. Saturdays were the day for leisure and sports; therefore it was allowed. I never understood the reasoning.

Within the Amish and some Mennonite groups clothing is what sets them apart; members can be recognized by their dress. A period of time was chosen as the most holy or appropriate and that became the standard. We have Pentecostals who dress like they walked out of the 1950's. And then we have the opposite extreme where in some churches clothes are almost optional.

To be legalistic in keeping laws whether they come from the Old Testament or Church law is damaging to our walk with Christ. My friend Nettie Musselman of South Carolina tells her story.

"I was born into a Mennonite family and while the church my family attended wasn't necessarily very conservative, my parents ended up sending us to a conservative Mennonite school when the Bible was taken out of public schools. I was in 5th grade at the time. I went from short hair and wearing pants to having to let my hair grow and wearing only dresses. As time went on, pressure was put on our family to attend church where our school was and at the age 15, after 2 years of instruction classes, I was baptized into the conservative Mennonite church and officially became a member there. For the next 16 years or so, I lived under the very strict rules of what is known as a conservative Mennonite church. The women and girls were required to wear coverings on their heads when they became Christians, and had to wear cape dresses with sleeves that came below the elbows and hems that had to be midway between the knee and ankle with simple patterns in the material. I learned to sew my own dresses and did my very best to stay within those guidelines. We also had to wear only black hosiery, socks and shoes—no sandals or any other footwear. Fear of disapproval from the ministry became a constant struggle. We were told this strict code of dress was designed to protect us. I lived in confusion and deep pain for years as a young girl, living this lifestyle, I was sexually molested. I wondered where I had gone wrong and what rules I might have disobeyed to have this happen to me.

I met and married my husband in the Mennonite church and for nine years we continued to attend that church. In 2006 we ended up leaving the Mennonite church, after my husband was excommunicated for confessing sin. We had a radical encounter with Jesus at that time and thus began our new and sometimes scary journey of learning how to make decisions without the church dictating to us what to do and wear. It was during this time we began hearing God for the first time-we were taught that God only spoke through the Bible and preachers. It is hard to describe the feelings I had when I realized that God didn't require me to dress a certain way to please Him! BLESSED FREEDOM! He wanted my heart, not a dress code! He heard me even when my head wasn't covered! He wanted a relationship with ME! Hallelujah!! It has continued to be a journey of learning more and more the true heart of my Father and walking out the things He shows me daily through His Spirit. He is not an angry God with a big stick, but a loving Father with a big heart!"

Thank you Nettie for sharing what happens when churches do not understand the new covenant. The amount of bondage, fear, control, anger, bitterness, and destroyed lives caused by bad theology is out of control. This is not why Jesus established a new covenant.

Why did clothes become a standard of holiness? Does it grow from a lack of revelation of the true nature of the new covenant? Why do we continually create rules which carry the illusion of spiritual maturity? Is it because we lack faith in the Holy Spirit?

The only reason I can think of as to why leaders attempt to enforce dress codes is because they are convinced most Christians will dress inappropriately if not given rules. Can the Holy Spirit lead believers as what clothes to wear? Do we really, as Christians, want to be defined as "those people 20 years behind in fashion?"

What about tattoos? Is this permitted for Christians? We cannot point to Leviticus 19 and demand obedience to the Mosaic Law, that is, unless we are committed to keeping the entire law. The same chapter where the law forbids 'tattoos' it also forbids wearing clothing of mixed cloth. Check your closet and throw out everything that is not 100% pure fiber. We cannot pick one law we like to enforce and ignore the rest.

4. Drinking Alcohol

If we went back in time—just several decades—this discussion was unheard of. Drinking any amount of alcohol by Christians was a sin and everyone knew it; especially the preachers. They lambasted drinking alcohol on a regular basis. In earlier times we (Evangelicals) were suspicious that traditional or liberal Christians drank, but discounted it because they were not "committed' believers." Now everything has changed. Today, it is not uncommon for Christians, even those attending Bible believing Evangelical Churches, to drink alcohol to some extent.

What does new covenant living say about drinking alcohol? Allow me to make two statements before exploring the Scriptures.

1. Drinking alcohol is not a sin.

2. Refraining from drinking alcohol is not a sin.

If we start here it will keep us from pointing our sharp little pointed fingers at our Christian sinners. If we enjoy drinking a glass of wine because we are free to do so and then assume our Christians friends who abstain are in bondage and need deliverance; we are wrong. If we hold to abstinence and think our friends who drink are turning their freedom into an opportunity for the flesh and are not mature in the use of freedom; we are wrong. The issue is not "to drink or not to drink" as much as our unhealthy attitude toward those holding a different view.

Alcohol in Scripture

Was the wine mentioned in the Bible (and other alcohol drinks) like ours today? Maybe it was just old grape juice they called wine. We see wine mentioned early in biblical history.

Genesis 14:18

After his return from the defeat of Chedorlaomer and the kings who were with him, the king of Sodom went out to meet him at the Valley of Shaveh (that is, the King's Valley). [18] And Melchizedek king of Salem brought out bread and wine. (He was priest of God Most High.)

"The Hebrew word translated wine in Genesis 14:18 is yayin. This word is used over 130 times in the Hebrew Bible to mean fermented wine, not grape juice. This same beverage, when used excessively, causes drunkenness. Genesis 9:21 says that Noah drank too much yayin and became drunk. Lot also became drunk on this beverage (Genesis 19:30-36), and so did Nabal (1 Samuel 25:36). Nevertheless, God told his people to enjoy yayin at the yearly festivals (Deuteronomy 14:26). In addition to using wine as a beverage, God also commanded the Levitical priests to include in the sacrifices a portion of wine (yayin) as a drink offering (Exodus 29:40)."[80]

If people got drunk on wine (yayin) in ancient times then we can be assured it was alcohol and not grape juice. What are the biblical warnings against drinking?

Proverbs 20:1

Wine is a mocker, strong drink a brawler,
and whoever is led astray by it is not wise.

---

[80] Grace Communion Internation-www.gci.org

Proverbs 23:29-31

Who has woe? Who has sorrow?
Who has strife? Who has complaining?
Who has wounds without cause?
Who has redness of eyes?

Those who tarry long over wine;
those who go to try mixed wine.
Do not look at wine when it is red,
when it sparkles in the cup
and goes down smoothly.

Proverbs 31:4

It is not for kings, O Lemuel,
it is not for kings to drink wine,
or for rulers to take strong drink.

Isaiah 5:11

Woe to those who rise early in the morning that they may
run after strong drink, who tarry late into the evening as
wine inflames them!

Ephesians 5:18

And do not get drunk with wine, for that is debauchery, but
be filled with the Spirit.

King James Version

And be not drunk with wine, wherein is excess; but be
filled with the Spirit;

The Message

Don't drink too much wine. That cheapens your life. Drink
the Spirit of God, huge draughts of him.

New American Standard Version

And do not get drunk with wine, for that is dissipation, but be filled with the Spirit.

We are told that too much wine causes "debauchery" (ESV), "excess," and "dissipation" (NASB). The Message says too much wine "cheapens your life." When there are a variety of English words I normally check in with Young's.

Young's Literal Translation

And be not drunk with wine, in which is dissoluteness, but be filled in the Spirit.

Not sure if "dissoluteness" helps out. Time for a dictionary.

Merriam-Webster

"Used to describe someone (such as a person who often gets drunk) whose way of living is considered morally wrong... Origin of dissolute-Middle English, from Latin *dissolutus,* from past participle of *dissolvere* to loosen, dissolve—First Known Use: 14th century."

To be drunk with wine then causes one to "loosen" to the degree of "excess" resulting in "debauchery." It is the path to losing one's passion for the Lord, to have the most important thing in your life flee away. It will steal your vision, your drive for life, and you end up far from your dreams.

I Timothy 3:8

Deacons likewise must be dignified, not double-tongued, not addicted to much wine, not greedy for dishonest gain.

Titus 2:3

Older women likewise are to be reverent in behavior, not slanderers or slaves to much wine.

Is there a case for abstaining from drinking wine or other forms of alcohol? We just read wine causes a person to become 'brawlers' will cause one to experience 'sorrow.' will lead to 'strife' and cause a person to 'complain.' It will 'cheapen your life.'

What is missing from those demanding total abstinence, is that Scripture never blames wine in itself for the problem. The problem is with the person doing the drinking. It is drinking *too much* wine. It is drinking to get drunk. The warning is for those who "run" after drink. Also, it never says drinking wine is a sin. As in most things, balance and moderation is needed.

Drinking wine is not a sin. Getting drunk may lead to sin. Therefore, the wise Christian must hold these in mind when making a decision to drink in a reasonable and moderate fashion.

The Case for Allowing Alcohol

Does the Bible allow drinking alcohol? The answer is yes. But it also provides common sense guidelines. A verse in the Old Testament should help in understanding this issue. The instructions are for celebrating during a Jewish feast.

Deuteronomy 14:26

And spend the money for whatever you desire—oxen or sheep or wine or strong drink, whatever your appetite craves. And you shall eat there before the LORD your God and rejoice, you and your household.

The context is the coming together at an annual gathering to bring the second tithe (tithe of celebration). If the journey was long they were to bring money and then buy what was desired—including wine and strong drink. There is no way around this—God instructed them to have a party. Their drinking was not off in private, it was not considered some indulgence of the flesh or sin. They were to enjoy their oxen or sheep barbecue and drink their wine before the Lord. Eating and drinking wine was a way to rejoice before their God.

Psalm 104:14-15

You cause the grass to grow for the livestock
and plants for man to cultivate,
that he may bring forth food from the earth
[15]and wine to gladden the heart of man,
oil to make his face shine
and bread to strengthen man's heart.

Wine is a gift from God to *"gladden the heart of man."*

In many fundamentalists circles it is taught Jesus never drank wine that contained alcohol. But think of a 1st Century wedding party where the host served grape juice. First of all, grape juice as we know it is a fairly recent innovation. When Paul told first century believers not to get drunk on wine, he was not thinking of grape juice. When the out-of-control Christians in Corinth were actually getting drunk at church he told them to eat and drink at home. According to Matthew 11:19, we know Jesus drank wine. Jesus' first miracle was making wine. Jesus compared the new covenant to that of new wine.

When we examine all words of Scripture concerning drinking wine and strong drink we find the key principle is to "not drink to excess." Do not get drunk and make a habit of drunkenness. It is time each side of the debate shows respect for those in disagreement. Stop holding up your version as the more spiritual and mature understanding. Acceptance and love will cover many bad attitudes in this situation.

Paul's advice may be useful here, *"So whatever you eat or drink, or whatever you do, do all to the glory of God* (I Cor. 10:31).

5. Abusive Church Leaders

When we understand grace in the new covenant our eyes open to abuses done in the name of Jesus. This is good—open eyes are better than closed ones—yet there are dangers in seeing with a fresh perspective. The first area of difficulty is controlling our first reaction which is often wrong. Bitterness, anger, and similar emotions often lead the way when we see what is going on behind the curtains. At this stage, there is only one possible action; wait and pray. The grace which opened our eyes now must work grace in our hearts toward those who abuse it. This is not easy.

We know there are leaders in churches who use manipulation, guilt, and threats to keep members loyal to their vision. It is an embarrassment to the church and in many of these situations there is nothing that can be done. They have built a structure around them where they cannot be touched. Pray for them and make a choice to live free.

As a former pastor I hesitate to approach this subject. The vast majority of pastors and leaders are wonderful servants of God doing their best to shepherd the church and be faithful stewards to their calling. They need support and encouragement. Being a pastor of a local church is difficult. One of my early spiritual fathers advised me about being called as a pastor. "If you can get out of it, do it; if you cannot, then you are called." This is sound advice. Being called as a pastor to oversee a local church is a great honor and a considerable challenge and no one should take it up unless the true call of God takes you captive.

There is no single advice for those under spiritual abuse. Each case is different. If there is opportunity for change from the inside, then work towards it. If everything is cast in stone with no visible change in sight then pray for a place where true ministers of the Gospel will shepherd you with the grace and love you deserve.

Apostle Peter gives great advice to church leaders and for us all:

I Peter 5:1-5

So I exhort the elders among you, as a fellow elder and a witness of the sufferings of Christ, as well as a partaker in the glory that is going to be revealed: [2] shepherd the flock of God that is among you, exercising oversight, not under compulsion, but willingly, as God would have you; not for shameful gain, but eagerly; [3] not domineering over those in your charge, but being examples to the flock. [4] And when the chief Shepherd appears, you will receive the unfading crown of glory. [5] Likewise, you who are younger, be subject to the elders. Clothe yourselves, all of you, with humility toward one another, for "God opposes the proud but gives grace to the humble.

I like how The Message words the first three verses:

I have a special concern for you church leaders. I know what it's like to be a leader, in on Christ's sufferings as well as the coming glory. Here's my concern: that you care for God's flock with all the diligence of a shepherd. Not because you have to, but because you want to please God. Not calculating what you can get out of it, but acting spontaneously. Not bossily telling others what to do, but tenderly showing them the way.

Our Glorious Covenant
New Start

As I finish writing the urge to hit delete and begin over is tempting. So much more needs to be said and said better. So many passages are yet to be explored in light of the new covenant. Greater wisdom and ability is needed for this complex yet rewarding subject. Nevertheless, this is offered to God's people as one place to start. Others are speaking, teaching, and releasing books which will add to this ongoing new covenant revolution.

I'm advocating a different path, a fourth way to understand the new covenant. My hope and prayer is this effort will help bring us closer to where we should be. Revelation of God's word is progressive. The next generation will see further and deeper than we did, and for that I rejoice.

We are building a system of biblical thought, a systematic way of viewing the story of redemptive history. We want a theology which frees people to walk in their destinies. We want the kingdom of God to advance. To make significant progress in our generation we cannot have people stuck in Egypt or wandering deserts. Freedom must be won. Freedom must be lived.

"For Freedom Christ has set you free; stand firm therefore, and do not submit again to a yoke of slavery (Apostle Paul, Gal.5:1).

Making final theological propositions must wait. It is far too early in our journey. After more books and articles are written, after much discussion and debate, we may arrive at a conclusion and a true statement of faith concerning covenant. We should not rush; we need time to develop a new way of thinking. I pray our heavenly Father will bless his church with passion for His presence and hunger for truth. Only in truth will we be free!

Even if our journey into new covenant truth is not complete, we can begin to see life changing practical principles.

1. Better Covenant Theology releases us from guilt, manipulation, coercion and fear.

2. Better Covenant Theology produces healthy Christians.

3. Better Covenant Theology with its emphasis upon the ever-increasing kingdom infuses optimism for the future

4. Better Covenant Theology simplifies life by following the Law of Christ.

5. Better Covenant Theology prioritizes relationships.

6. Better Covenant Theology creates a realistic-thinking people free of historical distortions (conspiracy theories).

7. Better Covenant Theology makes a joyful people.

8. Better Covenant Theology sees the whole of our lives as important and ends any spiritual versus secular divisions.

9. Better Covenant Theology creates balanced believers who are committed to their family, church and society without sacrificing one for the other.

10. Better Covenant Theology is the teaching of Jesus and the apostles that will transform the church.

11. Better Covenant Theology is 100% free of adherence to the Mosaic Law.

12. Better Covenant Theology emphasizes God's glory and our participation in the greatest delight in the world; enjoying his presence.

Appendix

613 Old Covenant Laws

1. To know that God exists (Ex. 20:2; Deut. 5:6)
2. Not to entertain the idea that there is any god but the Eternal (Ex. 20:3)
3. Not to blaspheme (Ex. 22:27-28) Lev 24:16
4. To hallow God's name (Lev. 22:32)
5. Not to profane God's name (Lev. 22:32
6. To know that God is One, a complete Unity (Deut. 6:4)
7. To love God (Deut. 6:5)
8. To fear Him reverently (Deut. 6:13; 10:20)
9. Not to put the word of God to the test (Deut. 6:16)
10. To imitate His good and upright ways (Deut. 28:9)

11. To honor the old and the wise (Lev. 19:32)
12. To learn Torah and to teach it (Deut. 6:7)
13. To cleave to those who know Him (Deut. 10:20)
14. Not to add to the commandments of the Torah (Deut.13:1)
15. Not to take away from the commandments of the Torah (Deut.13:1)
16. That every person shall write a scroll of the Torah for himself (Deut. 31:19)

17. To circumcise the male offspring (Gen. 17:12; Lev. 12:3)
18. To put fringes on the corners of clothing (Num. 15:38)
19. To bind God's Word on the head (Deut. 6:8)
20. To bind God's Word on the arm (Deut. 6:8)
21. To affix the mezuzah to the door posts and gates of your house (Deut. 6:9)

22. To pray to God (Ex. 23:25; Deut. 6:13)

23. To read the Shema [lit: The Hearing] in the morning and at night (Deut. 6:7)
24. To recite grace after meals (Deut. 8:10)
25. Not to lay down a stone for worship (Lev. 26:1)

26. To love all human beings who are of the covenant (Lev. 19:18)

27. Not to stand by idly when a human life is in danger (Lev. 19:16)

28. Not to wrong any one in speech (Lev. 25:17)

29. Not to carry tales (Lev. 19:16)

30. Not to cherish hatred in one's heart (Lev. 19:17)

31. Not to take revenge (Lev. 19:18)

32. Not to bear a grudge (Lev. 19:18)

33. Not to put any Jew to shame (Lev. 19:17)

34. Not to curse any other Israelite (Lev. 19:14)

35. Not to give occasion to the simple-minded to stumble on the road (Lev. 19:14) (this includes doing anything that will cause another to sin)

36. To rebuke the sinner (Lev. 19:17)

37. To relieve a neighbor of his burden and help to unload his beast (Ex. 23:5)

38. To assist in replacing the load upon a neighbor's beast (Deut.22:4)

39. Not to leave a beast, that has fallen down beneath its burden, unaided (Deut. 22:4)

40. Not to afflict an orphan or a widow (Ex. 22:21)

41. Not to reap the entire field (Lev. 19:9; Lev. 23:22)

42. To leave the unreaped corners of the field or orchard for the poor (Lev. 19:9)

43. Not to gather gleanings (the ears that have fallen to the ground while reaping)
(Lev. 19:9)

44. To leave the gleanings for the poor (Lev. 19:9)

45. Not to gather ol'loth (the imperfect clusters) of the vineyard (Lev. 19:10)

46. To leave ol'loth (the imperfect clusters) of the vineyard for the poor (Lev. 19:10; Deut. 24:21)

47. Not to gather the single grapes that have fallen to the ground (Lev. 19:10)

48. To leave the single grapes of the vineyard for the poor (Lev. 19:10)

49. Not to return to take a forgotten sheaf (Deut. 24:19) This applies to all fruit trees (Deut. 24:20)

50. To leave the forgotten sheaves for the poor (Deut. 24:19-20)

51. Not to refrain from maintaining a poor man and giving him what he needs (Deut. 15:7)

52. To give charity according to one's means (Deut. 15:11)

53. To love the stranger (Deut. 10:19) (CCA61).
54. Not to wrong the stranger in speech (Ex. 22:20)
55. Not to wrong the stranger in buying or selling (Ex. 22:20)
56. Not to intermarry with gentiles (Deut. 7:3)
57. To exact the debt of an alien (Deut. 15:3)
58. To lend to an alien at interest (Deut. 23:21)
59. To honor father and mother (Ex. 20:12)
60. Not to smite a father or a mother (Ex. 21:15)
61. Not to curse a father or mother (Ex. 21:17)
62. To reverently fear father and mother (Lev. 19:3)
63. To be fruitful and multiply (Gen. 1:28)
64. That a eunuch shall not marry a daughter of Israel (Deut. 23:2)
65. That a bastard [Heb. mamzer = illegitimate son] shall not marry the daughter of a Jew (Deut.23:3)
66. That an Ammonite or Moabite shall never marry the daughter of an Israelite (Deut. 23:4)

67. Not to exclude a descendant of Esau from the community of Israel for three generations (Deut. 23:8-9)
68. Not to exclude an Egyptian from the community of Israel for three generations (Deut. 23:8-9)
69. That there shall be no harlot (in Israel); that is, that there shall be no intercourse with a woman, without previous marriage with a deed of marriage and formal declaration of marriage (Deut.23:18)
70. To take a wife by the sacrament of marriage (Deut.24:1)
71. That the newly married husband shall (be free) for one year to rejoice with his wife (Deut. 24:5)
72. That a bridegroom shall be exempt for a whole year from taking part in any public labor, such as military service, guarding the wall and similar duties (Deut. 24:5)
73. Not to withhold food, clothing or conjugal rights from a wife (Ex. 21:10)
74. That the woman suspected of adultery shall be dealt with as prescribed in the Torah (Num. 5:30)
75. That one who defames his wife's honor (by falsely accusing her of unchastity before marriage) must live with her all his lifetime (Deut. 22:19)
76. That a man may not divorce his wife concerning whom he has published an evil report (about her unchastity before marriage) (Deut.

22:19)

77. To divorce by a formal written document (Deut. 24:1)

78. That one who divorced his wife shall not remarry her, if after the divorce she had been married to another man (Deut. 24:4)

79. That a widow whose husband died childless must not be married to anyone but her deceased husband's brother (Deut. 25:5) (this is only in effect insofar as it requires the procedure of release below).

80. To marry the widow of a brother who has died childless (Deut.25:5) (this is only in effect insofar as it requires the procedure of release below)

81. That the widow formally release the brother-in-law (if he refuses to marry her) (Deut. 25:7-9)

82. Not to indulge in familiarities with relatives, such as sensual kissing, carnal embracing, or provocative winking which may lead to incest (Lev.18:6)

83. Not to commit incest with one's mother (Lev. 18:7)

84. Not to commit sodomy with one's father (Lev. 18:7)

85. Not to commit incest with one's father's wife (Lev. 18:8)

86. Not to commit incest with one's sister (Lev. 18:9)

87. Not to commit incest with one's father's wife's daughter (Lev.18:9)

88. Not to commit incest with one's son's daughter (Lev. 18:10)

89. Not to commit incest with one's daughter's daughter (Lev.18:10)

90. Not to commit incest with one's daughter (this is not explicitly in the Torah but is inferred from other explicit commands that would include it)

91. Not to commit incest with one's fathers sister (Lev. 18:12)

92. Not to commit incest with one's mother's sister (Lev. 18:13)

93. Not to commit incest with one's father's brothers wife (Lev.18:14)

94. Not to commit sodomy with one's father's brother (Lev. 18:14)

95. Not to commit incest with one's son's wife (Lev. 18:15)

96. Not to commit incest with one's brother's wife (Lev. 18:16)

97. Not to commit incest with one's wife's daughter (Lev. 18:17)

98. Not to commit incest with the daughter of one's wife's son (Lev.18:17)

99. Not to commit incest with the daughter of one's wife's daughter (Lev. 18:17)

100. Not to commit incest with one's wife's sister (Lev. 18:18)

101. Not to have intercourse with a woman, in her menstrual period (Lev. 18:19)

102. Not to have intercourse with another man's wife (Lev. 18:20)

103. Not to commit sodomy with a male (Lev. 18:22)
104. Not to have intercourse with a beast (Lev. 18:23)
105. That a woman shall not have intercourse with a beast (Lev.18:23)
106. Not to castrate the male of any species; neither a man, nor a domestic or wild beast, nor a fowl (Lev. 22:24)

107. That the new month shall be solemnly proclaimed as holy, and the months and years shall be calculated by the Supreme Court only (Ex. 12:2)
108. Not to travel on the Sabbath outside the limits of one's place of residence (Ex. 16:29)
109. To sanctify the Sabbath (Ex. 20:8)
110. Not to do work on Sabbath (Ex. 20:10)
111. To rest on Sabbath (Ex. 23:12; 34:21)
112. To celebrate the festivals (Ex.23:14)
113. To rejoice on the festivals (Deut. 16:14)
114. To appear in the Sanctuary on the festivals (Deut. 16:16)
115. To remove leaven on the Eve of Passover (Ex. 12:15)
116. To rest on the first day of Passover (Ex. 12:16; Lev. 23:7)
117. Not to do work on the first day of Passover (Ex. 12:16; Lev.23:6-7)
118. To rest on the seventh day of Passover (Ex. 12:16; Lev. 23:8)
119. Not to do work on the seventh day of Passover (Ex. 12:16;Lev. 23:8)
120. To eat "matzah" [unleavened bread] on the first night of Passover (Ex. 12:18)
121. That no leaven be in the Israelite's possession during Passover (Ex. 12:19)
122. Not to eat any food containing leaven on Passover (Ex.12:20)
123. Not to eat leaven on Passover (Ex. 13:3)
124. That leaven shall not be seen in an Israelite's home during Passover (Ex. 13:7)

125. To discuss the departure from Egypt on the first night of Passover (Ex. 13:8)
126. Not to eat leaven after mid-day on the fourteenth of Nissan (Deut. 16:3)
127. To count forty-nine days from the time of the cutting of the Omer (i.e. first sheaves of the barley harvest) (Lev. 23:15)

128. To rest on Pentecost (Lev. 23:21)

129. Not to do work on the feast of Pentecost (Lev. 23:21)

130. To rest on Rosh Hashanah [i.e. the feast of Trumpets] (Lev. 23:24) (CCA29)

131. Not to do work on Rosh Hashanah (Lev. 23:25)

132. To hear the sound of the Trumpet [Heb. shofar or ram's horn] (Num. 29:1)

133. To fast on Yom Kippur i.e. the day of Atonement (Lev. 23:27)

134. Not to eat or drink on Yom Kippur (Lev. 23:29) (CCN152)

135. Not to do work on Yom Kippur (Lev. 23:31) (CCN151)

136. To rest on the Yom Kippur (Lev. 23:32)

137. To rest on the first day of the feast of Tabernacles or Booths.[Heb. Sukkot] (Lev. 23:35)

138. Not to do work on the first day of the feast of Tabernacles. (Lev. 23:35)

139. To rest on the eighth day of the feast of Tabernacles (Lev.23:36)

140. Not to do work on the eighth day of the feast of Tabernacles (Lev. 23:36)

141. To take during Sukkot a palm branch and the other three plants (Lev. 23:40)

142. To dwell in booths seven days during Sukkot (Lev. 23:42)

143. To examine the marks in cattle (so as to distinguish the clean from the unclean) (Lev. 11:2)

144. Not to eat the flesh of unclean beasts (Lev. 11:4)

145. To examine the marks in fishes (so as to distinguish the clean from the unclean (Lev. 11:9)

146. Not to eat unclean fish (Lev. 11:11)

147. To examine the marks in fowl, so as to distinguish the clean from the unclean (Deut. 14:11)

148. Not to eat unclean fowl (Lev. 11:13)

149. To examine the marks in locusts, so as to distinguish the clean from the unclean (Lev. 11:21)

150. Not to eat a worm found in fruit (Lev. 11:41)

151. Not to eat of things that creep upon the earth (Lev. 11:41-42)

152. Not to eat any vermin of the earth (Lev. 11:44)

153. Not to eat things that swarm in the water (Lev. 11:43 and 46)

154. Not to eat of winged insects (Deut. 14:19)

155. Not to eat the flesh of a beast that is torn (Ex.22:30)

156. Not to eat the flesh of a beast that died of itself (Deut. 14:21)
157. To slay cattle, deer and fowl according to the law if their flesh is to be eaten (Deut. 12:21)
158. Not to eat a limb removed from a living beast (Deut. 12:23)
159. Not to slaughter an animal and its young on the same day (Lev.22:28)
160. Not to take the mother-bird with the young (Deut. 22:6)
161. To set the mother-bird free when taking the nest (Deut.22:6-7)
162. Not to eat the flesh of an ox that was condemned to be stoned (Ex. 21:28)
163. Not to boil meat with milk (Ex. 23:19)
164. Not to eat flesh with milk (Ex. 34:26)
165. Not to eat the of the thigh-vein which shrank (Gen. 32:33)
166. Not to eat the fat of the offering (Lev. 7:23)
167. Not to eat blood (Lev. 7:26)
168. To cover the blood of undomesticated animals (deer, etc.) and of fowl that have been killed (Lev. 17:13)

169. Not to eat or drink like a glutton or a drunkard (not to rebel against father or mother) (Lev. 19:26; Deut. 21:20)

170. Not to do wrong in buying or selling (Lev. 25:14)
171. Not to make a loan to an Israelite on interest (Lev. 25:37)
172. Not to borrow on interest (Deut. 23:20) (because this would cause the lender to sin)
173. Not to take part in any usurious transaction between borrower and lender, neither as a surety, nor as a witness, nor as a writer of the bond for them (Ex. 22:24)
174. To lend to a poor person (Ex. 22:24)
175. Not to demand from a poor man repayment of his debt, when the creditor knows that he cannot pay, nor press him (Ex.22:24)
176. Not to take in pledge utensils used in preparing food (Deut.24:6)
177. Not to exact a pledge from a debtor by force (Deut. 24:10)
178. Not to keep the pledge from its owner at the time when he needs it (Deut. 24:12)
179. To return a pledge to its owner (Deut. 24:13)
180. Not to take a pledge from a widow (Deut. 24:17)
181. Not to commit fraud in measuring (Lev. 19:35)
182. To ensure that scales and weights are correct (Lev. 19:36)
183. Not to possess inaccurate measures and weights (Deut.25:13-14)

184. Not to delay payment of a hired man's wages (Lev. 19:13)

185. That the hired laborer shall be permitted to eat of the produce he is reaping (Deut. 23:25-26)

186. That the hired laborer shall not take more than he can eat (Deut. 23:25)

187. That a hired laborer shall not eat produce that is not being harvested (Deut. 23:26)

188. To pay wages to the hired man at the due time (Deut. 24:15)

189. To deal judicially with the Hebrew bondman in accordance with the laws appertaining to him (Ex. 21:2-6)

190. Not to compel the Hebrew servant to do the work of a slave (Lev. 25:39)

191. Not to sell a Hebrew servant as a slave (Lev. 25:42)

192. Not to treat a Hebrew servant rigorously (Lev. 25:43)

193. Not to permit a gentile to treat harshly a Hebrew bondman sold to him (Lev. 25:53)

194. Not to send away a Hebrew bondman servant empty handed, when he is freed from service (Deut. 15:13)

195. To bestow liberal gifts upon the Hebrew bondsman (at the end of his term of service), and the same should be done to a Hebrew bondwoman (Deut. 15:14)

196. To redeem a Hebrew maid-servant (Ex. 21:8)

197. Not to sell a Hebrew maid-servant to another person (Ex. 21:8)

198. To espouse a Hebrew maid-servant (Ex. 21:8-9)

199. To keep the Canaanite slave forever (Lev. 25:46)

200. Not to surrender a slave, who has fled to the land of Israel, to his owner who lives outside Palestine (Deut. 23:16)

201. Not to wrong such a slave (Deut. 23:17)

202. Not to muzzle a beast, while it is working in produce which it can eat and enjoy (Deut. 25:4)

203. That a man should fulfill whatever he has uttered (Deut. 23:24)

204. Not to swear needlessly (Ex. 20:7)

205. Not to violate an oath or swear falsely (Lev. 19:12)

206. To decide in cases of annulment of vows, according to the rules set forth in the Torah (Num. 30:2-17)

207. Not to break a vow (Num. 30:3)

208. To swear by His name truly (Deut. 10:20)

209. Not to delay in fulfilling vows or bringing vowed or free-will offerings (Deut. 23:22)

210. To let the land lie fallow in the Sabbatical year (Ex. 23:11; Lev.25:2)
211. To cease from tilling the land in the Sabbatical year (Ex. 23:11) (Lev. 25:2)
212. Not to till the ground in the Sabbatical year (Lev. 25:4)
213. Not to do any work on the trees in the Sabbatical year (Lev.25:4)
214. Not to reap the aftermath that grows in the Sabbatical year, in the same way as it is reaped in other years (Lev. 25:5)
215. Not to gather the fruit of the tree in the Sabbatical year in the same way as it is gathered in other years (Lev. 25:5)
216. To sound the Ram's horn in the Sabbatical year (Lev. 25:9)
217. To release debts in the seventh year (Deut. 15:2)
218. Not to demand return of a loan after the Sabbatical year has passed (Deut. 15:2)
219. Not to refrain from making a loan to a poor man, because of the release of loans in the Sabbatical year (Deut. 15:9)
220. To assemble the people to hear the Torah at the close of the seventh year (Deut. 31:12)
221. To count the years of the Jubilee by years and by cycles of seven years (Lev. 25:8)
222. To keep the Jubilee year holy by resting and letting the land lie fallow (Lev. 25:10)
223. Not to cultivate the soil nor do any work on the trees, in the Jubilee Year (Lev. 25:11)
224. Not to reap the aftermath of the field that grew of itself in the Jubilee Year, in the same way as in other years (Lev. 25:11)
225. Not to gather the fruit of the tree in the Jubilee Year, in the same way as in other years (Lev. 25:11)
226. To grant redemption to the land in the Jubilee year (Lev. 25:24)

227. To appoint judges and officers in every community of Israel (Deut. 16:18)
228. Not to appoint as a judge, a person who is not well versed in the laws of the Torah, even if he is expert in other branches of knowledge (Deut. 1:17)
229. To adjudicate cases of purchase and sale (Lev. 25:14)
230. To judge cases of liability of a paid depositary (Ex. 22:9)

231. To adjudicate cases of loss for which a gratuitous borrower is liable (Ex. 22:13-14)

232. To adjudicate cases of inheritances (Num. 27:8-11)

233. To judge cases of damage caused by an uncovered pit (Ex.21:33-34)

234. To judge cases of injuries caused by beasts (Ex. 21:35-36)

235. To adjudicate cases of damage caused by trespass of cattle (Ex.22:4)

236. To adjudicate cases of damage caused by fire (Ex. 22:5)

237. To adjudicate cases of damage caused by a gratuitous depositary (Ex. 22:6-7)

238. To adjudicate other cases between a plaintiff and a defendant (Ex. 22:8)

239. Not to curse a judge (Ex. 22:27)

240. That one who possesses evidence shall testify in Court (Lev.5:1)

241. Not to testify falsely (Ex. 20:13)

242. That a witness, who has testified in a capital case, shall not lay down the law in that particular case (Num. 35:30)

243. That a transgressor shall not testify (Ex. 23:1)

244. That the court shall not accept the testimony of a close relative of the defendant in matters of capital punishment (Deut. 24:16)

245. Not to hear one of the parties to a suit in the absence of the other party (Ex. 23:1)

246. To examine witnesses thoroughly (Deut. 13:15)

247. Not to decide a case on the evidence of a single witness (Deut.19:15)

248. To give the decision according to the majority, when there is a difference of opinion among the members of the Sanhedrin as to matters of law (Ex. 23:2)

249. Not to decide, in capital cases, according to the view of the majority, when those who are for condemnation exceed by one only, those who are for acquittal (Ex. 23:2)

250. That, in capital cases, one who had argued for acquittal, shall not later on argue for condemnation (Ex. 23:2)

251. To treat parties in a litigation with equal impartiality (Lev. 19:15)

252. Not to render iniquitous decisions (Lev. 19:15)

253. Not to favor a great man when trying a case (Lev. 19:15)

254. Not to take a bribe (Ex. 23:8)

255. Not to be afraid of a bad man, when trying a case (Deut. 1:17)

256. Not to be moved in trying a case, by the poverty of one of the

parties (Ex. 23:3; Lev. 19:15)

257. Not to pervert the judgment of strangers or orphans (Deut.24:17)

258. Not to pervert the judgment of a sinner (a person poor in fulfillment of commandments) (Ex. 23:6)

259. Not to render a decision on one's personal opinion, but only on the evidence of two witnesses, who saw what actually occurred (Ex. 23:7)

260. Not to execute one guilty of a capital offense, before he has stood his trial (Num. 35:12)

261. To accept the rulings of every Supreme Court in Israel (Deut. 17:11)

262. Not to rebel against the orders of the Court (Deut. 17:11)

263. To make a parapet for your roof (Deut. 22:8)

264. Not to leave something that might cause hurt (Deut. 22:8)

265. To save the pursued even at the cost of the life of the pursuer (Deut. 25:12)

266. Not to spare a pursuer, but he is to be slain before he reaches the pursued and slays the latter, or uncovers his nakedness (Deut. 25:12)

267. Not to sell a field in the land of Israel in perpetuity (Lev. 25:23)

268. Not to change the character of the open land (about the cities of) the Levites or of their fields; not to sell it in perpetuity, but it may be redeemed at any time (Lev. 25:34)

269. That houses sold within a walled city may be redeemed within a year (Lev. 25:29)

270. Not to remove landmarks (property boundaries) (Deut. 19:14)

271. Not to swear falsely in denial of another's property rights (Lev.19:11)

272. Not to deny falsely another's property rights (Lev. 19:11)

273. Never to settle in the land of Egypt (Deut. 17:16)

274. Not to steal personal property (Lev. 19:11)

275. To restore that which one took by robbery (Lev. 5:23)

276. To return lost property (Deut. 22:1)

277. Not to pretend not to have seen lost property, to avoid the obligation to return it (Deut. 22:3)

278. Not to slay an innocent person (Ex. 20:13)

279. Not to kidnap any person of Israel (Ex. 20:13)

280. Not to rob by violence (Lev. 19:13)

281. Not to defraud (Lev. 19:13)

282. Not to covet what belongs to another (Ex. 20:14)

283. Not to crave something that belongs to another (Deut. 5:18)
284. Not to indulge in evil thoughts and sights (Num. 15:39)

285. That the Court shall pass sentence of death by decapitation with the sword (Ex. 21:20; Lev. 26:25)
286. That the Court shall pass sentence of death by strangulation (Lev. 20:10)
287. That the Court shall pass sentence of death by burning with fire (Lev. 20:14)
288. That the Court shall pass sentence of death by stoning (Deut.22:24)

289. To hang the dead body of one who has incurred that penalty (Deut. 21:22)
290. That the dead body of an executed criminal shall not remain hanging on the tree overnight (Deut. 21:23)
291. To inter the executed on the day of execution (Deut. 21:23)
292. Not to accept ransom from a murderer (Num. 35:31)
293. To exile one who committed accidental homicide (Num. 35:25)
294. To establish six cities of refuge (for those who committed accidental homicide) (Deut. 19:3)
295. Not to accept ransom from an accidental homicide, so as to relieve him from exile (Num. 35:32)
296. To decapitate the heifer in the manner prescribed (in expiation of a murder on the road, the perpetrator of which remained undiscovered) (Deut. 21:4)
297. Not to plow nor sow the rough valley (in which a heifer's neck was broken) (Deut. 21:4)
298. To adjudge a thief to pay compensation or (in certain cases) suffer death (Ex. 21:16; Ex. 21:37; Ex. 22:1)
299. That he who inflicts a bodily injury shall pay monetary compensation (Ex. 21:18-19)
300. To impose a penalty of fifty shekels upon the seducer (of an unbetrothed virgin) and enforce the other rules in connection with the case (Ex. 22:15-16)
301. That the violator (of an unbetrothed virgin) shall marry her (Deut. 22:28-29)
302. That one who has raped a damsel and has then (in accordance with the law) married her, may not divorce her (Deut. 22:29)
303. Not to inflict punishment on the Sabbath (Ex. 35:3) (because some punishments were inflicted by fire)

304. To punish the wicked by the infliction of stripes (Deut. 25:2)

305. Not to exceed the statutory number of stripes laid on one who has incurred that punishment (Deut. 25:3) (and by implication, not to strike anyone)

306. Not to spare the offender, in imposing the prescribed penalties on one who has caused damage (Deut. 19:13)

307. To do unto false witnesses as they had purposed to do (to the accused) (Deut. 19:19)

308. Not to punish anyone who has committed an offense under duress (Deut. 22:26)

309. To heed the call of every prophet in each generation, provided that he neither adds to, nor takes away from the Torah (Deut.18:15)

310. Not to prophesy falsely (Deut. 18:20)

311. Not to refrain from putting a false prophet to death nor to be in fear of him (Deut. 18:22) (negative)

312. Not to make a graven image; neither to make it oneself nor to have it made by others (Ex. 20:4)

313. Not to make any figures for ornament, even if they are not worshipped (Ex. 20:20)

314. Not to make idols even for others (Ex. 34:17; Lev. 19:4)

315. Not to use the ornament of any object of idolatrous worship (Deut. 7:25)

316. Not to make use of an idol or its accessory objects, offerings, or libations (Deut. 7:26)

317. Not to drink wine of idolaters (Deut. 32:38)

318. Not to worship an idol in the way in which it is usually worshipped (Ex. 20:5)

319. Not to bow down to an idol, even if that is not its mode of worship (Ex. 20:5)

320. Not to prophesy in the name of an idol (Ex. 23:13; Deut.18:20)

321. Not to hearken to one who prophesies in the name of an idol (Deut. 13:4)

322. Not to lead the children of Israel astray to idolatry (Ex. 23:13)

323. Not to entice an Israelite to idolatry (Deut. 13:12)

324. To destroy idolatry and its appurtenances (Deut. 12:2-3)

325. Not to love the enticer to idolatry (Deut. 13:9)

326. Not to give up hating the enticer to idolatry (Deut. 13:9)

327. Not to save the enticer from capital punishment, but to stand by at his execution (Deut. 13:9)

328. A person whom he attempted to entice to idolatry shall not urge pleas for the acquittal of the enticer (Deut. 13:9)

329. A person whom he attempted to entice shall not refrain from giving evidence of the enticer's guilt, if he has such evidence (Deut. 13:9)

330. Not to swear by an idol to its worshipers, nor cause them to swear by it (Ex. 23:13)

331. Not to turn one's attention to idolatry (Lev. 19:4)

332. Not to adopt the institutions of idolaters nor their customs (Lev. 18:3; Lev. 20:23)

333. Not to pass a child through the fire to Molech (Lev. 18:21)

334. Not to suffer any one practicing witchcraft to live (Ex. 22:17)

335. Not to practice observing times or seasons -i.e. astrology (Lev. 19:26)

336. Not to practice superstitions/witchcraft (doing things based on signs and potions; using charms and incantations) (Lev. 19:26)

337. Not to consult familiar spirits or ghosts (Lev. 19:31)

338. Not to consult wizards (Lev. 19:31)

339. Not to practice specific magic by using stones herbs or objects. (Deut. 18:10)

340. Not to practice magical practices in general.(Deut. 18:10)

341. Not to practice the art of casting spells over snakes and scorpions (Deut. 18:11)

342. Not to enquire of a familiar spirit or ghost (Deut. 18:11)

343. Not to seek the dead (Deut. 18:11)

344. Not to enquire of a wizard (Deut. 18:11)

345. Not to remove the entire beard, like the idolaters (Lev. 19:27)

346. Not to round the corners of the head, as the idolatrous priests do (Lev. 19:27)

347. Not to cut oneself or make incisions in one's flesh in grief, like the idolaters (Lev. 19:28; Deut. 14:1)

348. Not to tattoo the body like the idolaters (Lev. 19:28)

349. Not to make a bald spot for the dead (Deut. 14:1)

350. Not to plant a tree for worship (Deut. 16:21)

351. Not to set up a pillar (for worship) (Deut. 16:22)

352. Not to show favor to idolaters (Deut. 7:2)

353. Not to make a covenant with the seven (Canaanite, idolatrous) nations (Ex. 23:32; Deut. 7:2)

354. Not to settle idolaters in our land (Ex. 23:33)

355. To slay the inhabitants of a city that has become idolatrous and burn that city (Deut. 13:16-17)

356. Not to rebuild a city that has been led astray to idolatry (Deut.13:17)

357. Not to make use of the property of city that has been so led astray (Deut. 13:18)

358. Not to cross-breed cattle of different species (Lev. 19:19)

359. Not to sow different kinds of seed together in one field (Lev.19:19)

360. Not to eat the fruit of a tree for three years from the time it was planted (Lev. 19:23)

361. That the fruit of fruit-bearing trees in the fourth year of their planting shall be sacred like the second tithe and eaten in Jerusalem (Lev. 19:24)

362. Not to sow grain or herbs in a vineyard (Deut. 22:9)

363. Not to eat the produce of diverse seeds sown in a vineyard (Deut. 22:9)

364. Not to work with beasts of different species, yoked together (Deut. 22:10)

365. That a man shall not wear women's clothing (Deut. 22:5)

366. That a woman should not wear men's clothing (Deut. 22:5)

367. Not to wear garments made of wool and linen mixed together (Deut. 22:11)

368. To redeem the firstborn human male (Ex. 13:13; Ex. 34:20; Num. 18:15)

369. To redeem the firstling of an ass (Ex. 13:13; Ex. 34:20)

370. To break the neck of the firstling of an ass if it is not redeemed (Ex. 13:13; Ex. 34:20)

371. Not to redeem the firstling of a clean beast (Num. 18:17)

372. That the Priest shall put on priestly vestments for the service (Ex. 28:2)

373. Not to tear the High Priest's robe (Ex. 28:32)

374. That the Priest shall not enter the Sanctuary at all times (i.e., at times when he is not performing service) (Lev. 16:2)

375. That the ordinary Priest shall not defile himself by contact with any dead, other than immediate relatives (Lev. 21:1-3)

376. That the sons of Aaron defile themselves for their deceased relatives

(by attending their burial), and mourn for them like other Israelites, who are commanded to mourn for their relatives (Lev.21:3)

377. That a Priest who had an immersion during the day (to cleanse him from his uncleanness) shall not serve in the Sanctuary until after sunset (Lev. 21:6)

378. That a Priest shall not marry a divorced woman (Lev. 21:7)

379. That a Priest shall not marry a harlot (Lev. 21:7)

380. That a Priest shall not marry a profaned woman (Lev. 21:7)

381. To show honor to a Priest, and to give him precedence in all things that are holy (Lev. 21:8)

382. That a High Priest shall not defile himself with any dead, even if they are relatives (Lev. 21:11)

383. That a High Priest shall not go (under the same roof) with a dead body (Lev. 21:11)

384. That the High Priest shall marry a virgin (Lev. 21:13)

385. That the High Priest shall not marry a widow (Lev. 21:14)

386. That the High Priest shall not cohabit with a widow, even without marriage, because he profanes her (Lev. 21:15)

387. That a person with a physical blemish shall not serve (in the Sanctuary) (Lev. 21:17)

388. That a Priest with a temporary blemish shall not serve there (Lev. 21:21)

389. That a person with a physical blemish shall not enter the Sanctuary further than the altar (Lev. 21:23)

390. That a Priest who is unclean shall not serve (in the Sanctuary) (Lev. 22:2-3)

391. To send the unclean out of the Camp, that is, out of the Sanctuary (Num. 5:2)

392. That a Priest who is unclean shall not enter the courtyard (Num. 5:2-3) This refers to the Camp of the Sanctuary

393. That the sons or descendants of Aaron shall bless Israel (Num. 6:23)

394. To set apart a portion of the dough for the Priest (Num.15:20)

395. That the Levites shall not occupy themselves with the service that belongs to the sons of Aaron, nor the sons of Aaron with that belonging to the Levites (Num. 18:3)

396. That one not a descendant of Aaron in the male line shall not serve (in the Sanctuary) (Num. 18:4-7)

397. That the Levite shall serve in the Sanctuary (Num. 18:23)

398. To give the Levites cities to dwell in, these to serve also as cities of refuge (Num. 35:2)

399. That none of the tribe of Levi shall take any portion of territory in the land (of Israel) (Deut. 18:1)

400. That none of the tribe of Levi shall take any share of the spoil (at the conquest of the Promised Land) (Deut. 18:1)

401. That the sons of Aaron shall serve in the Sanctuary in divisions, but on festivals, they all serve together (Deut. 18:6-8)

402. That an uncircumcised person shall not shall not eat of the t'rumah (heave offering), and the same applies to other holy things. This rule is inferred from the law of the Paschal offering, by similarity of phrase (Ex. 12:44-45 and Lev. 22:10) but it is not explicitly set forth in the Torah. Traditionally, it has been learnt that the rule that the uncircumcised must not eat holy things is an essential principle of the Torah and not an enactment of the Scribes

403. Not to alter the order of separating the t'rumah and the tithes; the separation be in the order first-fruits at the beginning, then the t'rumah, then the first tithe, and last the second tithe (Ex. 22:28)

404. To give half a shekel every year (to the Sanctuary for provision of the public sacrifices) (Ex. 30:13)

405. That a priest [kohein] who is unclean shall not eat of the t'rumah (Lev. 22:3-4)

406. That a person who is not a kohein or the wife or unmarried daughter of a kohein shall not eat of the t'rumah (Lev. 22:10)

407. That a sojourner with a kohein or his hired servant shall not eat of the t'rumah (Lev. 22:10)

408. Not to eat unholy things [Heb. tevel] (something from which the t'rumah and tithe have not yet been separated) (Lev. 22:15)

409. To set apart the tithe of the produce (one tenth of the produce after taking out t'rumah) for the Levites (Lev. 27:30; Num. 18:24)

410. To tithe cattle (Lev. 27:32)

411. Not to sell the tithe of the heard (Lev. 27:32-33)

412. That the Levites shall set apart a tenth of the tithes, which they had received from the Israelites, and give it to the Priest [Heb. kohanim] (called the t'rumah of the tithe) (Num. 18:26)

413. Not to eat the second tithe of cereals outside Jerusalem (Deut. 12:17)

414. Not to consume the second tithe of the vintage outside of Jerusalem (Deut. 12:17)

415. Not to consume the second tithe of the oil outside of Jerusalem (Deut. 12:17)

416. Not to forsake the Levites (Deut. 12:19); but their gifts (dues) should be given to them, so that they might rejoice therewith on each and every festival

417. To set apart the second tithe in the first, second, fourth and fifth years of the sabbatical cycle to be eaten by its owner in Jerusalem (Deut. 14:22)

418. To set apart the second tithe in the third and sixth year of the sabbatical cycle for the poor (Deut. 14:28-29)

419. To give the kohein [i.e. Priest] the due portions of the carcass of cattle (Deut. 18:3)

420. To give the first of the fleece to the priest (Deut. 18:4)

421. To set apart a small portion of the grain, wine and oil for the Priest [Heb. kohein] [Heb. t'rumah g'dolah i.e.(the great heave-offering) (Deut. 18:4)

422. Not to expend the proceeds of the second tithe on anything but food and drink (Deut. 26:14)

423. Not to eat the Second Tithe, even in Jerusalem, in a state of uncleanness, until the tithe had been redeemed (Deut. 26:14)

424. Not to eat the Second Tithe, when mourning (Deut. 26:14)

425. To make the declaration, when bringing the second tithe to the Sanctuary (Deut. 26:13)

426. Not to build an altar of hewn stone (Ex. 20:22)

427. Not to mount the altar by steps (Ex. 20:23)

428. To build the Sanctuary (Ex. 25:8)

429. Not to remove the staves from the Ark (Ex. 25:15)

430. To set the showbread and the frankincense before the Lord every Sabbath (Ex. 25:30)

431. To kindle lights in the Sanctuary (Ex. 27:21)

432. That the breastplate shall not be loosened from the ephod (Ex.28:28)

433. To offer up incense twice daily (Ex. 30:7)

434. Not to offer strange incense nor any sacrifice upon the golden altar (Ex. 30:9)

435. That the Priest shall wash his hands and feet at the time of service (Ex. 30:19)

436. To prepare the oil of anointment and anoint high priests and kings

with it (Ex. 30:31)

437. Not to compound oil for lay use after the formula of the anointing oil (Ex. 30:32-33)

438. Not to anoint a stranger with the anointing oil (Ex. 30:32)

439. Not to compound anything after the formula of the incense (Ex.30:37)

440. That he who, in error, makes unlawful use of sacred things, shall make restitution of the value of his trespass and add a fifth (Lev. 5:16)

441. To remove the ashes from the altar (Lev. 6:3)

442. To keep fire always burning on the altar of the burnt-offering (Lev. 6:6)

443. Not to extinguish the fire on the altar (Lev. 6:6)

444. That a kohein shall not enter the Sanctuary with disheveled hair (Lev. 10:6)

445. That a kohein shall not enter the Sanctuary with torn garments (Lev. 10:6)

446. That the kohein shall not leave the Courtyard of the Sanctuary, during service (Lev. 10:7)

447. That an intoxicated person shall not enter the Sanctuary nor give decisions in matters of the Law (Lev. 10:9-11)

448. To revere the Sanctuary (Lev. 19:30) (today, this applies to synagogues)

449. That when the Ark is carried, it should be carried on the shoulder (Num. 7:9)

450. To observe the second Passover (Num. 9:11)

451. To eat the flesh of the Paschal lamb on it, with unleavened bread and bitter herbs (Num. 9:11)

452. Not to leave any flesh of the Paschal lamb brought on the second Passover until the morning (Num. 9:12)

453. Not to break a bone of the Paschal lamb brought on the second Passover (Num. 9:12)

454. To sound the trumpets at the offering of sacrifices and in times of trouble (Num. 10:9-10)

455. To watch over the edifice continually (Num. 18:2)

456. Not to allow the Sanctuary to remain unwatched (Num. 18:5)

457. That an offering shall be brought by one who has in error committed a trespass against sacred things, or robbed, or lain carnally with a bond-maid betrothed to a man, or denied what was deposited with him and swore falsely to support his denial. This is called a guilt-offering for a

known trespass (Lev. 5:15-19)

458. Not to destroy anything of the Sanctuary, of synagogues, or of houses of study, nor erase the holy names (of God); nor may sacred scriptures be destroyed (Deut. 12:2-4)

459. To sanctify the firstling of clean cattle and offer it up (Ex. 13:2; Deut. 15:19)

460. To slay the Paschal lamb (Ex. 12:6)

461. To eat the flesh of the Paschal sacrifice on the night of the fifteenth of Nissan (Ex. 12:8)

462. Not to eat the flesh of the Paschal lamb raw or sodden (Ex. 12:9)

463. Not to leave any portion of the flesh of the Paschal sacrifice until the morning unconsumed (Ex. 12:10)

464. Not to give the flesh of the Paschal lamb to an Israelite who had become an apostate (Ex. 12:43)

465. Not to give flesh of the Paschal lamb to a stranger who lives among you to eat (Ex. 12:45)

466. Not to take any of the flesh of the Paschal lamb from the company's place of assembly (Ex. 12:46)

467. Not to break a bone of the Paschal lamb (Ex. 12:46)

468. That the uncircumcised shall not eat of the flesh of the Paschal lamb (Ex. 12:48)

469. Not to slaughter the Paschal lamb while there is leaven in the home (Ex. 23:18; Ex. 24:25)

470. Not to leave the part of the Paschal lamb that should be burnt on the altar until the morning, when it will no longer be fit to be burnt (Ex. 23:18; Ex. 24:25)

471. Not to go up to the Sanctuary for the festival without bringing an offering (Ex. 23:15)

472. To bring the first fruits to the Sanctuary (Ex. 23:19)

473. That the flesh of a sin-offering and guilt-offering shall be eaten (Ex. 29:33)

474. That one not of the seed of Aaron, shall not eat the flesh of the holy sacrifices (Ex. 29:33)

475. To observe the procedure of the burnt-offering (Lev. 1:3)

476. To observe the procedure of the meal-offering (Lev. 2:1)

477. Not to offer up leaven or honey (Lev. 2:11)

478. That every sacrifice be salted (Lev. 2:13)

479. Not to offer up any offering unsalted (Lev. 2:13)
480. That the Court of Judgment shall offer up a sacrifice if they have erred in a judicial pronouncement (Lev. 4:13)
481. That an individual shall bring a sin-offering if he has sinned in error by committing a transgression (Lev. 4:27-28)
482. To offer a sacrifice of varying value in accordance with one's means (Lev. 5:7)
483. Not to sever completely the head of a fowl brought as a sin-offering (Lev. 5:8)
484. Not to put olive oil in a sin-offering made of flour (Lev. 5:11)
485. Not to put frankincense on a sin-offering made of flour (Lev.5:11)
486. That an individual shall bring an offering if he is in doubt as to whether he has committed a sin for which one has to bring a sin-offering. (Lev.5:17-19)
487. That the remainder of the meal offerings shall be eaten (Lev. 6:9)
488. Not to allow the remainder of the meal offerings to become leavened (Lev. 6:10)
489. That the High Priest [Heb. Kohein] shall offer a meal offering daily (Lev. 6:13)
490. Not to eat of the meal offering brought by Aaron and his sons (Lev. 6:16)

491. To observe the procedure of the sin-offering (Lev. 6:18)
492. Not to eat of the flesh of sin offerings, the blood of which is brought within the Sanctuary and sprinkled towards the Veil (Lev. 6:23)
493. To observe the procedure of the guilt-offering (Lev. 7:1)
494. To observe the procedure of the peace-offering (Lev. 7:11)
495. To burn meat of the holy sacrifice that has remained over (Lev. 7:17)
496. Not to eat of sacrifices that are eaten beyond the appointed time for eating them (Lev. 7:18)
497. Not to eat of holy things that have become unclean (Lev. 7:19)
498. To burn meat of the holy sacrifice that has become unclean (Lev. 7:19)
499. That a person who is unclean shall not eat of things that are holy (Lev. 7:20)
500. A Priest's daughter who profaned herself shall not eat of the holy things, neither of the heave offering nor of the breast, nor of the shoulder of peace offerings (Lev. 10:14, Lev. 22:12)

501. That a woman after childbirth shall bring an offering when she is clean (Lev. 12:6)

502. That the leper shall bring a sacrifice after he is cleansed (Lev.14:10)

503. That a man having an issue shall bring a sacrifice after he is cleansed of his issue (Lev. 15:13-15)

504. That a woman having an issue shall bring a sacrifice after she is cleansed of her issue (Lev. 15:28-30)

505. To observe, on Yom Kippur, the service appointed for that day, regarding the sacrifice, confessions, sending away of the scapegoat, etc. (Lev. 16:3-34)

506. Not to slaughter beasts set apart for sacrifices outside (the Sanctuary) (Lev. 17:3-4)

507. Not to eat flesh of a sacrifice that has been left over (beyond the time appointed for its consumption) (Lev. 19:8)

508. Not to sanctify blemished cattle for sacrifice on the altar (Lev. 22:20) This text prohibits such beasts being set apart for sacrifice on the altar

509. That every animal offered up shall be without blemish (Lev. 22:21)

510. Not to inflict a blemish on cattle set apart for sacrifice (Lev. 22:21)

511. Not to slaughter blemished cattle as sacrifices (Lev. 22:22)

512. Not to burn the limbs of blemished cattle upon the altar (Lev. 22:22)

513. Not to sprinkle the blood of blemished cattle upon the altar (Lev. 22:24)

514. Not to offer up a blemished beast that comes from non-Israelites (Lev. 22:25)

515. That sacrifices of cattle can only take place when they are at least eight days old (Lev. 22:27)

516. Not to leave any flesh of the thanksgiving offering until the morning (Lev. 22:30)

517. To offer up the meal-offering of the Omer on the morrow after the first day of Passover, together with one lamb (Lev. 23:10)

518. Not to eat bread made of new grain before the Omer of barley has been offered up on the second day of Passover (Lev. 23:14)

519. Not to eat roasted grain of the new produce before that time (Lev. 23:14)

520. Not to eat fresh ears of the new grain before that time (Lev. 23:14)

521. To bring on wave loaves of bread together with the sacrifices which are then offered up in connection with the loaves [Pentecost feast] (Lev.

23:17-20)
522. To offer up an additional sacrifice on Passover (Lev. 23:36)
523. That one who vows to the Lord the monetary value of a person shall pay the amount appointed in the Scriptural portion (Lev. 27:2-8)
524. If a beast is exchanged for one that had been set apart as an offering, both become sacred (Lev. 27:10)
525. Not to exchange a beast set aside for sacrifice (Lev. 27:10)
526. That one who vows to the Lord the monetary value of an unclean beast shall pay its value (Lev. 27:11-13)

527. That one who vows the value of a his house shall pay according to the appraisal of the Priest (Lev. 27:11-13)
528. That one who sanctifies to the Lord a portion of his field shall pay according to the estimation appointed in the Scriptural portion (Lev. 27:16-24)
529. Not to transfer a beast set apart for sacrifice from one class of sacrifices to another (Lev. 27:26)
530. To decide in regard to dedicated property as to which is sacred to the Lord and which belongs to the Priest (Lev. 27:28)

531. Not to sell a field devoted to the Lord (Lev. 27:28)

532. Not to redeem a field devoted to the Lord (Lev. 27:28)

533. To make confession before the Lord of any sin that one has committed, when bringing a sacrifice and at other times (Num.5:6-7)

534. Not to put olive oil in the meal-offering of a woman suspected of adultery (Num. 5:15)

535. Not to put frankincense on it (Num. 5:15)

536. To offer up the regular sacrifices daily (two lambs as burnt offerings) (Num. 28:3)

537. To offer up an additional sacrifice every Sabbath (two lambs) (Num. 28:9)

538. To offer up an additional sacrifice every New Moon (Num. 28:11)

539. To bring an additional offering on the day of the first fruits [Pentecost] (Num. 28:26-27)

540. To offer up an additional sacrifice on [Feast of Trumpets] or Rosh Hashanah (Num.29:1-6)

541. To offer up an additional sacrifice on the day of Atonement or Yom Kippur (Num. 29:7-8)

542. To offer up an additional sacrifice on Feast of Tabernacles [Heb. Sukkot] (Num. 29:12-34)

543. To offer up an additional offering on the eighth day after the feast of Tabernacles called (Heb. Shemini Atzeret), which is a festival by itself (Num. 29:35-38) This eighth day is an anticipation of the New Testament Sabbath which would be instituted on the first day of the week, which is also the eighth day.

544. To bring all offerings, whether obligatory or freewill, on the first festival after these were incurred (Deut. 12:5-6)

545. Not to offer up sacrifices outside (the Sanctuary) (Deut. 12:13)

546. To offer all sacrifices in the Sanctuary (Deut. 12:14)

547. To redeem cattle set apart for sacrifices that contracted disqualifying blemishes, after which they may be eaten by anyone. (Deut. 12:15)

548. Not to eat of the unblemished firstling outside Jerusalem (Deut. 12:17)

549. Not to eat the flesh of the burnt-offering (Deut. 12:17). This is a Prohibition applying to every trespasser, not to enjoy any of the holy things.

550. That the sons of Aaron [i.e. his descendants] shall not eat the flesh of the sin-offering or guilt-offering outside the Courtyard (of the Sanctuary) (Deut. 12:17)

551. Not to eat of the flesh of the sacrifices that are holy in a minor degree, before the blood has been sprinkled (on the altar), (Deut. 12:17)

552. That the Priest shall not eat the first-fruits before they are set down in the Courtyard (of the Sanctuary) (Deut. 12:17)

553. To take trouble to bring sacrifices to the Sanctuary from places outside the land of Israel (Deut. 12:26)

554. Not to eat the flesh of beasts set apart as sacrifices, that have been rendered unfit to be offered up by deliberately inflicted blemish (Deut. 14:3)

555. Not to do work with cattle set apart for sacrifice (Deut. 15:19)

556. Not to shear beasts set apart for sacrifice (Deut. 15:19)

557. Not to leave any portion of the festival offering brought on the fourteenth of Nissan unto the third day (Deut. 16:4)

558. Not to offer up a beast that has a temporary blemish (Deut. 17:1)

559. Not to bring sacrifices out of the hire of a harlot or price of a dog (apparently a euphemism for sodomy) (Deut. 23:19)

560. To read the portion prescribed on bringing the first fruits (Deut. 26:5-10)

561. That eight species of creeping things defile by contact (Lev. 11:29-30)

562. That foods become defiled by contact with unclean things (Lev. 11:34)

563. That anyone who touches the carcass of a beast that died of itself shall be unclean (Lev. 11:39)

564. That a lying-in woman is unclean like a menstruating woman (in terms of uncleanness) (Lev. 12:2-5)

565. That a leper is unclean and defiles (Lev. 13:2-46)

566. That the leper shall be universally recognized as such by the prescribed marks So too, all other unclean persons should declare themselves as such (Lev. 13:45)

567. That a leprous garment is unclean and defiles (Lev. 13:47-49)

568. That a leprous house defiles (Lev. 14:34-46)

569. That a man, having a running issue, defiles (Lev. 15:1-15)

570. That the seed of copulation defiles (Lev. 15:16)

571. That purification from all kinds of defilement shall be effected by ceremonial washing (Lev. 15:16)

572. That a menstruating woman is unclean and defiles others (Lev. 15:19-24)

573. That a woman, having a running issue, defiles (Lev. 15:25-27)

574. To carry out the ordinance of the Red Heifer so that its ashes will always be available (Num. 19:9)

575. That a corpse defiles (Num. 19:11-16)

576. That the waters of separation defile one who is clean, and cleanse the unclean from pollution by a dead body (Num. 19:19-22

577. Not to drove off the hair of the scull (Lev. 13:33)

578. That the procedure of cleansing leprosy, whether of a man or of a house, takes place with cedar-wood, hyssop, scarlet thread, two birds, and running water (Lev. 14:1-7)

579. That the leper shall shave all his hair (Lev. 14:9)

580. Not to pluck out the marks of leprosy (Deut. 24:8)

581. Not to curse a ruler, that is, the King in the land of Israel (Ex. 22:27)

582. To appoint a king (Deut. 17:15)

583. Not to appoint as ruler over Israel, one who comes from non-Israelites (Deut. 17:15)

584. That the King shall not acquire an excessive number of horses (Deut. 17:16)

585. That the King shall not take an excessive number of wives (Deut. 17:17)

586. That he shall not accumulate an excessive quantity of gold and silver (Deut. 17:17)

587. That the King shall write a scroll of the Torah for himself, in addition to the one that every person should write, so that he writes two scrolls (Deut. 17:18)

588. That a Nazarite shall not drink wine, or anything mixed with wine which tastes like wine; and even if the wine or the mixture has turned sour, it is prohibited to him (Num. 6:3)

589. That he shall not eat fresh grapes (Num. 6:3)

590. That he shall not eat dried grapes (raisins) (Num. 6:3)

591. That he shall not eat the kernels of the grapes (Num. 6:4)

592. That he shall not eat of the skins of the grapes (Num. 6:4)

593. That the Nazarite shall permit his hair to grow (Num. 6:5)

594. That the Nazarite shall not cut his hair (Num. 6:5)

595. That he shall not enter any covered structure where there is a dead body (Num. 6:6)

596. That a Nazarite shall not defile himself for any dead person (by being in the presence of the corpse) (Num. 6:7)

597. That the Nazarite shall shave his hair when he brings his offerings at the completion of the period of his Nazariteship, or within that period if he has become defiled (Num. 6:9)

598. That those engaged in warfare shall not fear their enemies nor be panic-stricken by them during battle (Deut. 3:22, 7:21,20:3)

599. To anoint a special Priest (to speak to the soldiers) in a war (Deut.

20:2) This is today's equivalent to a military chaplain.

600. In a permissive war (as distinguished from obligatory ones), to observe the procedure prescribed in the Torah (Deut. 20:10)

601. Not to keep alive any individual of the seven Canaanite nations (Deut. 20:16)

602. To exterminate the seven Canaanite nations from the land of Israel (Deut. 20:17)

603. Not to destroy fruit trees (wantonly or in warfare) (Deut. 20:19-20)

604. To deal with a beautiful woman taken captive in war in the manner prescribed in the Torah (Deut. 21:10-14)

605. Not to sell a beautiful woman, (taken captive in war) (Deut. 21:14)

606. Not to degrade a beautiful woman (taken captive in war) to the condition of a bondwoman (Deut. 21:14)

607. Not to offer peace to the Ammonites and the Moabites before waging war on them, as should be done to other nations (Deut. 23:7)

608. That anyone who is unclean shall not enter the Camp of the Levites (Deut. 23:11)

609. To have a place outside the camp for sanitary purposes (Deut. 23:13)

610. To keep that place sanitary (Deut. 23:14-15)

611. Always to remember what Amalek did (Deut. 25:17)

612. That the evil done to us by Amalek shall not be forgotten (Deut. 25:19)

613. To destroy the seed of Amalek (Deut. 25:19)

Books by Stan Newton

Glorious Kingdom
A Handbook on Partial Preterist Eschatology

Glorious Kingdom is a comprehensive book on eschatology; kingdom eschatology. In this book Stan Newton takes on dispensational eschatology, which is the position of many evangelicals and lays a foundation from Scripture for a different view. Glorious Kingdom covers all major aspects of eschatology with special emphasis on interpreting the prophetic New Testament passages from the viewpoint of the kingdom of God. The kingdom was established by Jesus in the first century. This book will help those seeking biblical answers to tough questions on eschatology.

Soon coming books by Stan Newton:

Breakfast in Tel-Aviv
A Conversation about Replacement Theology

Shane recently graduated from a Pentecostal Bible school. His future was secure within his denomination except one very large adjustment; his changed his theology. After finishing seminary he moves back near his hometown church and former pastor to begin his ministry. Pastor George is waiting for answers. Over coffee the question is asked, "Shane, you have not abandoned Israel, have you?"

Breakfast in Tel-Aviv is the story of Pastor Shane and Pastor George as they share their positions on Israel. Emotions are high as they regularly discuss their views. Their discussions lead to a trip to Israel and over breakfast all is resolved; or is it?

Kingdom Communion
The Mystery of the Fourth Cup

Many in Pentecostal/Charismatic churches are getting burned out by an overly subjective worship. Kingdom Communion is written with the conviction that the Lord's Supper must return to its proper place in our regular worship services. Why are many Churches neglecting the Lord's Table? Is it because our 'communion service' is more like a funeral than a wedding? Stan Newton addresses the historical beliefs and then offers something different; viewing communion from a kingdom and eschatological position. When Jesus as the 'son of man' came in his kingdom to end one age and begin a new age-the kingdom age-then, our understanding of communion must change. When will Jesus drink the fourth cup with us?

CPSIA information can be obtained
at www.ICGtesting.com
Printed in the USA
FSOW02n2013280217
31398FS

9 781615 291595